A THEATRE FOR EVERYBODY

The Old Vic · May 1942 ·

The Old Vic after a raid — from a painting by Roger Furse

A THEATRE
FOR EVERYBODY

THE STORY OF
THE OLD VIC AND SADLER'S WELLS

BY EDWARD J. DENT

ILLUSTRATED BY KAY AMBROSE

LONDON AND NEW YORK
T. V. BOARDMAN AND COMPANY LIMITED
14 COCKSPUR STREET, LONDON, SW1

FIRST PUBLISHED 1945

BOOK
PRODUCTION
WAR ECONOMY
STANDARD

*This book is produced in complete
conformity with the authorised
economy standards*

SET IN 11 ON 12 MONOTYPE GARAMOND

Made and printed in England by
STAPLES PRESS LIMITED
at their St. Albans, Herts, factory

CONTENTS

PREFACE

THE HISTORY of the Old Vic and Sadler's Wells Theatres has already been written several times. This history falls naturally into two well-defined parts divided by the dates at which the management of these theatres was taken over by Miss Cons and Miss Baylis respectively. Sadler's Wells Theatre is the older of the two, having been built towards the end of the seventeenth century; the building now known as the Old Vic was erected in 1816 and opened in 1818. It passed into the hands of Miss Cons in 1880; her niece Miss Baylis succeeded to the management in 1897 and Sadler's Wells, which had long stood derelict, was once more rebuilt and reopened as an 'Old Vic for North London' under her direction in 1931. The early history of the two theatres is really inseparable from the history of the London stage in general; Miss Cons's management hardly belongs to theatrical history at all – it was an experiment in philanthropy. The history of the Old Vic as a new force in the dramatic life of London did not begin until 1914, and although opera had been established there much earlier than drama, what took place under that category at the Old Vic was little more than a prelude to the developments which were eventually to make the name of Sadler's Wells the acknowledged symbol of all that was most progressive in the production of opera in English, as well as of an art of ballet, essentially English in character, and so peculiarly typical of our own time as to amount almost to a newly created form of entertainment.

Historians of these two theatres have hitherto tended to treat the subject as if Sadler's Wells and the Royal Cobourg were for the most part quite exceptional in the entertainments which they presented. The period of Miss Cons has been generally ignored, as it offered little or no opportunity for amusing anecdote. With the advent of Miss Baylis there confronts us a personality so outstandingly unique that one can hardly be surprised if those who worked under her felt compelled to write more about her own individual self than about the achievements of her theatre. It may well be asked what need there is for any further book on the two theatres to be written. I have no desire to hash up once more the anecdotes which have been so agreeably and instructively presented in the two books of Mr. Edwin Fagg; I need hardly say that I am deeply indebted to them. Nor can I compete with Dame Sybil Thorndike and her brother in painting the portrait of Miss Baylis. But it is now eight years since Miss Baylis died. People said at that time that the Vic and Wells were bound to come to an end, since no one could ever replace that singular combination of artistic insight and ignorance, personal goodness and hard-headed business capacity. None the less, the two theatres have continued their work and have prospered. At the moment of writing the disasters of war have thrown both buildings out of action; there were indeed moments when it was feared that all their activities, wherever they might have found a temporary home, would have to remain at best in suspended animation, if not to perish for ever. But a new era is in sight; whatever changes the future may bring, there can be no doubt that all three departments of the Vic-Wells organisation, Drama, Opera and Ballet, are flourishing and full of vitality in spite of all the practical difficulties with which they have to contend.

For Miss Cons the Vic was merely 'her recreation' and little more than an attraction to a coffee tavern, just as the first 'musick house' at Sadler's Wells was no more than an inducement to take a drive and a drink of medicinal waters. Miss Baylis had the vision of a really national theatre. Whether this country will ever achieve a State-subsidised National Theatre and National Opera in English is a question to which few of us would dare to conjecture an answer; but it has for some time been becoming clear to all serious lovers of music and drama that Miss Baylis had come nearer to achieving the realisation of that vision than any of the various bodies set up to consider possibilities. It did not matter to her whether her theatres were State-subsidised or not, and she certainly would have resented furiously any sort of Ministerial interference with her own personal management. But she was quite aware, I think, that she was already setting a very good example of what the State ought to have undertaken long ago.

During the General Election of 1929 members of the British Drama League were invited by the committee of the League to ask Parliamentary candidates if they would pledge themselves to support a reasonable grant for a National Theatre, if and when the question was raised in the next Parliament. The magazine *Drama* printed an interesting specimen of the replies received.

The Conservative candidate replied that while in sympathy with the arts there would be no funds available for such a purpose. The audience received the question and answer with laughter. The Liberal candidate said that he thought he could say yes. The audience received the question and answer in silence. The Labour candidate replied emphatically 'Yes', and devoted five minutes to explaining the need for a National Theatre and a National Opera. The audience received the question and answer with applause. The sender of this information deduced from it (1) that the Labour candidate was the only one of the three who had given thought to the question before it was put to him; (2) that the Labour audience was the only one alive to the fact that a National Theatre would aid the culture of the people.

The reader may be interested to learn that the Conservative candidate on this occasion was the Right Honourable Winston Churchill.

The relation of the theatre to the nation is a social question. Miss Cons was first and foremost a social reformer. I propose therefore to consider in the following chapters the social conditions of the theatre in this country which gradually led up to the state of affairs which Miss Cons felt called upon to sweep away. Her work in the theatre was mainly destructive, and if she had had collaborators enough to carry out her principles to the end, she might have effected the complete annihilation of the British drama. Her niece Lilian Baylis had a more constructive imagination. Miss Cons cleared the ground, Miss Baylis laid the foundations of new movements. She did not create the National Theatre, and she was far from being the only contributor towards the National Theatre movement. The whole national outlook on the theatre, including opera as well as drama, has undergone a complete change during the last fifty years, and to write the history of this transformation would be a task far beyond my own powers and beyond the scope of this particular book. Miss Cons probably never realised what she herself had initiated; to her mind, as far as one who never knew her can judge, opera and drama were things of far less importance than coffee and lemonade. Miss Baylis, like Moses, saw no more than the vision of the Promised Land; I deliberately adopt this trite and hackneyed allusion because I think it is just what would have appealed seriously to her profoundly religious mind. Like Moses, she was a great leader; but it must be remembered, not only by her actual successors in her two theatres, but by all who have the cause of British Drama and Opera at heart, that her work will be of no avail unless every one of us resolves to contribute whatever we can towards its continuance and expansion.

This is not an appeal for money. The problem of the National Theatre is not to be solved by a Government subsidy alone, still less by the establishment of a Ministry of Fine Arts; it is primarily a matter of goodwill and personal devotion from all sorts and conditions of men and women.

My most cordial thanks are due to the Governors of the Royal Victoria Hall Foundation for kindly placing at my disposal their records and minute-books; to the late Sir William Rothenstein for kindly allowing me to reproduce his drawings of Miss Cons and Miss Baylis; to Mr. Tyrone Guthrie, Miss Muriel Gough, Miss Joan Cross, Miss Evelyn Williams, and Mrs. Thellusson for pictures, photographs and much information and general help; to Mr. Geoffrey Whitworth and to Miss Coates, Librarian of the British Drama League; to Mr. W. Bridges Adams; to Major Robert Medley for permission to reproduce his prize design for the safety curtain at the Old Vic, now destroyed; to Mr. C. T. Smith for photograph of *The Magic Flute* in the Isle of Dogs; and finally to Mr. Lawrence Haward for valuable criticism.

London, February, 1945

WHAT HAS always struck the Continental visitor to England as pre-eminently characteristic of our national outlook on life is our sense of historical continuity. In most other countries there survives the memory of some national revolution, and whether it be as remote as the French Revolution now appears to us, or as recent as those which have taken place in Germany, Italy or Spain, the tendency is to regard this date as the beginning of all things and to forget as far as possible whatever may have happened before it. We had a 'glorious revolution' in England, too, but the most glorious thing about it was that it was accomplished without bloodshed and indeed so quietly that history seems hardly to have been aware of it at all; the average man, indeed, for whom history is just '1066 and all that' would probably be quite unable to say when it happened or what it destroyed. The foreigner obviously notes our continuity in the numberless odd customs that have survived all over the country; but the truest continuity of our culture is to be found in our language and in our literature, above all in our drama, of which Shakespeare is naturally the great symbolic figure. There was a time, and that not so very long ago, when it could be said that the Bible was the one book which every Englishman knew; to-day that has notoriously ceased to be true. What we may call 'general utility' language is more likely to quote *Alice in Wonderland* than Holy Scripture; but if there is one writer who still stands safe and unshaken, it is Shakespeare, and it must be borne in mind that Shakespeare is inseparable from the theatre. It is the theatre which has taught us all those turns of phrase which by now have become more like unavoidable idioms of speech than familiar quotations; and not only the theatre of Shakespeare himself, but the theatre of many now forgotten dramatists, including the most trivial manufacturers of melodrama, farce and burlesque.

If we are tracing the history of the theatre itself, Shakespeare gives us at once our most obvious line of continuity. Every student of the drama knows Professor Odell's monumental work, *Shakespeare from Betterton to Irving;* and there is material for almost as large a book on the Shakespeare performances which have taken place since Irving died. It may be wondered, however, whether the modern playgoer would feel completely at home if he could hear and see an exact reproduction of *Hamlet* as played by Irving, Macready, Edmund Kean, John Philip Kemble or Garrick, and we may be quite sure that the modern playgoer, whatever he thought of the great actor's interpretations, would have been completely bewildered and revolted by the behaviour of audiences that was habitual from the days of Betterton almost down to those of Irving in such a theatre as Drury Lane, to say nothing of what went on down to the days of Miss Cons in a lower class of entertainment. The older generation of writers on dramatic history devoted themselves mainly either to a study of drama considered as literature, or to the biography of the great actors and actresses; it is only recently that learned researchers like Professor Allardyce Nicoll and the Rev. Montague Summers have investigated both the structural and mechanical appurtenances of the theatre and the social aspects of the theatre, its daily life, its economics and its audiences.

The modern English theatre may be said to begin at the Restoration, when women were first allowed to appear professionally on the public stage, and when the stage began gradually but systematically to adopt the principle of a proscenium limiting the stage like a picture frame and exhibiting scenery painted in perspective. Before the closing of the theatres during the Commonwealth the new Italian scenery had been shown only in the Court masques, and it was only in these that ladies had appeared as amateur actresses or dancers. The Restoration theatre did not abolish the platform stage entirely; what we now call the apron extended to a distance represented by the width of at least two, and sometimes three, side boxes. As late as 1841 this vast apron and its adjacent side boxes remained in existence at Her Majesty's Theatre, which had been rebuilt after various fires on the site of Vanbrugh's Italian Opera Theatre erected in 1705. These boxes were sometimes within and sometimes outside the main curtain; they are seen clearly in Hogarth's painting of *The Beggar's Opera*, and boxes within the curtain existed until quite recently at the Paris Opera. In Restoration days it was still unusual for the orchestra to be placed in front of the stage, where we are accustomed to find it now; this was done only for performances which approximated to operas. But the 'music-room' above the stage disappeared by the beginning of the eighteenth century, and the present position of the orchestra then became normal. The pit extended right up to the orchestra, or to the stage itself if the musicians were above; reserved stalls were not introduced until 1829, and then only at the Italian Opera – naturally enough, since we may read in various travel books of the period that English visitors to Italy were surprised and gratified to find such conveniences in the opera houses of Naples.

The Restoration theatre, as Professor Nicoll points out, was much more like a private theatre of the Italian Renaissance than like the Elizabethan theatre, in that its audience was almost exclusively limited to the society which frequented the Court. This did not make that audience any the better behaved; the pit was always full of young men of fashion, shouting, roaring, quarrelling and brawling, disturbing the performance without any consideration, and playing all sorts of rough practical jokes. The orange-women bawled their wares all over the house, and the theatre in all its departments was the regular resort of the ladies of easy virtue. No woman of reputation could show her face in the pit, although it was very common for society ladies to move about there wearing masks in order to engage the young gentlemen in adventurous conversation. This was another practice common in Italy, especially at carnival time. Charles II seems himself to have made the order that no spectators were to be allowed on the stage; in the Elizabethan theatre it had, of course, been the recognised custom that the best people sat on stools on the stage itself. When

The best people sat on stools on the stage itself

the stage became more of a picture-stage and scenery more elaborate it was obviously a great hindrance to the performance to have a large number of spectators encumbering it. But the wings and the back rooms were always easy of access, and we find Pepys and his friends constantly behind the scenes and on terms of the closest intimacy with the leading actresses. A few years after the death of Charles II the practice of sitting on the stage itself had become general again, and the nuisance was not done away with until the reign of Queen Anne.

During the course of the following century and for the first forty years of the nineteenth it has to be borne in mind that the performance of what was called 'the legitimate drama' was strictly limited to the privileged houses or 'patent theatres', as they were called – eventually to the two great theatres in Drury Lane and Covent

Garden. Until the passing of the Theatre Regulation Act in 1843 these two houses (and their predecessors of an earlier age) were the only places in London licensed for the performance of Shakespeare and the entire repertory of normal tragedy and comedy. This meant that until 1843 all the other theatres of London and the suburbs were of a very miscellaneous character, approximating more to music-halls and variety entertainments.

Quite apart from all these there stood the Italian Opera House; it had been built by Vanbrugh for Betterton and his dramatic company and was first opened in 1705, but owing to the Italianate magnificence of its architecture it was found acoustically impossible for the spoken drama. It was, however, ideally suited to opera, especially to opera sung by Italians in their own language, and having a special licence of its own it remained the home of Italian opera until 1887; it was finally pulled down in 1891. Another reason for its becoming an Italian opera house was the choice of site. A new large theatre in any city generally has to be built on the outskirts where open ground is available; the gradual growth of Berlin can be traced in the sites of its chief theatres, each new one having been erected further and further from the original centre of the town. In 1705 the Haymarket was too far away from the residential quarters of London for those who had to walk, as well as being dangerous at night; consequently the public for that theatre was pretty well limited to those rich enough to drive there in their own coaches and carriages. The Italian Opera has for two hundred years and more been a very important yet strange feature of London's theatrical and social life; we shall revert to it in a later chapter of this book.

Sadler's Wells is the oldest theatre in London which still preserves something of the original structure. The mineral spring from which it takes its name was discovered in 1683 and exploited by one Sadler as a rival to the already fashionable wells of Tunbridge and Epsom. For this purpose he built a music house in which performances of various kinds were given by singers, acrobats and dancers. This was the natural beginning for any place of entertainment, and we can observe the same thing in a later generation when Miss Cons opened her reformed Old Vic with ballad concerts. Plays did not come until later, and in the case of Sadler's Wells legitimate drama could not make its appearance until after the passing of the Theatre Regulation Act. Tate Wilkinson, the famous manager of the York circuit during the latter half of the eighteenth century, gives an amusing account of the first play ever acted at Harrogate, which throws a curious light on the attitude of the provincial public to the theatre. This was in 1774; the Harrogate waters did not become fashionable until well on into the eighteenth century. The play was advertised to begin at half-past six, but the local population was so unaccustomed to entertainments that began at a definite hour that when the curtain was due to rise there was only one person in the theatre, a Mr. Moody, himself an actor. The musicians played *Britons, strike home* and the play began, but most of the audience did not arrive until about an hour later, when they were much taken aback to find that the play was half over. We need not be surprised then to learn that the audience at Sadler's Wells was as disorderly as at any other theatre. Islington in those days was one of the many villages on the outer fringes of London to which people resorted to frequent the pleasure-gardens, and Sadler's Wells was a good deal nearer to what was then the residential part of London than it is now to such quarters as Bayswater, Kensington and Chelsea. In 1743 the gardens passed into the possession of a man called Rosoman, who considerably developed the place as a scene of entertainment. The medicinal waters went out of fashion, but the gradual extension of London made it worth Rosoman's while to rebuild the wooden music-house as a regular theatre in brick. This was finished in 1765; Rosoman's name is commemorated by Rosoman Street which now crosses Rosebery Avenue at the Finsbury Town Hall. By this time the theatre could be carried on with considerable popular success, but only with entertainments of comparatively humble character, and it was notorious as the meeting-place of highwaymen and pickpockets. Tate Wilkinson in 1786 and 1787 engaged tumblers (i.e. acrobats) from Sadler's Wells for the Doncaster theatre during the time of the races. For many years one of the chief attractions there was the famous clown Joseph Grimaldi, who has been immortalised by the collaboration of Charles Dickens and George Cruikshank; later on the theatre was managed by the Dibdin family, under whom the stage was reconstructed as a huge tank full of water supplied from the New River, in which aquatic spectacles and all sorts of nautical melodramas were performed. It was the period of Nelson's victories, and the battle-pieces represented at Sadler's Wells fulfilled exactly the same requirements for that generation as the war-propaganda films do for certain types of audience to-day. All historians have been forced to admit and to lament the steady decadence of the English theatre from the early eighteenth century down to Victorian days; in the course of this book we shall have occasion to consider this decadence from various points of view. The theatres provided what the public wanted, and if we compare the miscellaneous entertainments of a hundred and fifty years ago with those of to-day we shall soon become aware that there is very little difference between the general taste of the two ages. Modern audiences have learned to behave better; but ridiculous as the patriotic melodramas and the sentimental comic operas of those days may appear to the modern reader, especially when viewed by means of the quaint illustrations of Cruikshank and of Pollock's Juvenile Theatre, it is obvious that the real theatre of the present day has only benefited by the transference of its less educated audiences to the cinemas.

The change in manners dates from the reign of Queen Victoria. Throughout the eighteenth century there were perpetually recurring riots in the theatres, even in the privileged houses. As long as the pit reached right up to the edge of the stage it was always possible for the disorderly occupants to clamber over the orchestra barrier and on to the stage itself, assault the actors and destroy the scenery whenever they thought they had cause of quarrel. Eventually it became the rule in all theatres for the orchestra barrier to be surmounted by a row of sharp iron spikes. The noisy people of the Restoration had been the young gentlemen of the nobility, and in many succeeding generations their descendants kept up the practice of turbulence in the theatre. Their seniors were less violent, but often quite annoying enough. Garrick had to reprimand Dr. Johnson for talking loudly in a side box during the most tragic moments of *King Lear;* Hazlitt at a later date describes the nuisance of the elderly gentlewomen who chattered all through the plays at the Haymarket. But the audiences of the eighteenth century were no longer mainly aristocratic. A new middle class was springing up and beginning to frequent the theatres more and more; the pit and gallery were always full of a rabble that only too often made it impossible to hear what the actors were saying. Some critics laid the blame on the large houses, others on the small; a small house invited familiarities with the actors, and a large one, with its vast reverberations, gave every encouragement to noise for its own sake.

Between 1826 and 1829 Prince Pückler-Muskau, a German nobleman, paid extensive visits to the British Isles; his letters from this country were first published in Germany and appeared in an English translation in 1832. The Prince was naturally received in the best society, and so much of his book is taken up with descriptions of country-house life that the translator felt obliged to curtail these drastically as being information quite superfluous for his English readers. For the reader of to-day the most interesting sections of the Prince's memoirs are those which deal with the theatre. It must be borne in mind that he was an enthusiastic admirer of most things English, and especially of the great English actors of that date; if we quote certain passages of severe disapproval these must be read as exceptional and therefore all the more deserving of credence.

One of his expeditions was to Sadler's Wells.

'JUNE 16, 1827. I went to a little theatre, as yet unknown to me, called Sadler's Wells, which is a good three-quarters of a mile from my dwelling.* I went in a hackney coach. When I wanted to go home, towards one o'clock, I could find no coach in this out-of-the-way place, and all the houses were shut. This was the more disagreeable, as I had really not the least idea in what part of the town I was.

* The author reckons in German miles; as a German mile was equal to four-and-two-thirds of an English mile, the distance would be three-and-a-half English miles.

'After wandering about the streets in vain for half-an-hour in search of a coach, I resigned myself to the idea of finding my way home on foot, with the aid of a watchman, when a stage coach came by which was going my way, and with which I happily regained my Penates about two o'clock. The peculiarity of this theatre is that it contains real water, in which element the actors splash and dabble about by the hour together, like ducks or water-rats; *au reste* nothing can surpass the nonsense of the melodrame, nor the horror of the singing by which it was accompanied.'

Even now Sadler's Wells is none too easy of access. It would be attractive to quote the Prince's long and elaborate description of *Punch and Judy* seen in the streets, which he evidently enjoyed immensely, and rightly thought the most typically English of all dramas, but it would not be relevant to our subject. There are other aspects of English character on which we must hear his views.

'The most striking thing to a foreigner in English theatres is the unheard-of coarseness and brutality of the audiences. The consequence of this is that the higher and more civilised classes go only to the Italian Opera, and very rarely visit their national theatre. Whether this be unfavourable or otherwise to the stage I leave others to determine.

'English freedom here degenerates into the rudest licence, and it is not uncommon in the midst of the most affecting part of a tragedy, or in the most charming *cadenza* of a singer to hear some coarse expression shouted from the galleries in stentor voice. This is followed, according to the taste of the bystanders, either by loud laughter and approbation, or by the castigation and expulsion of the offender. Whichever turn the thing takes, you can hear no more of what is passing on the stage, where actors and singers, according to ancient usage, do not suffer themselves to be interrupted by such occurrences, but declaim or warble away, *comme si rien n'était*. And such things happen not once, but sometimes twenty times, in the course of a performance, and amuse many of the audience more than that does. It is also no rarity for someone to throw the fragments of his *goûté*, which do not always consist of orange-peel alone, without the smallest ceremony on the heads of the people in the pit, or to shail* them with singular dexterity into the boxes, while others hang their coats and waistcoats over the railing of the gallery and sit in shirt-sleeves; in short, all that could be devised for the better excitement of a phlegmatic *Harmonie* society of the workmen in Berlin under the renowned Wisostsky is to be found in the national theatre of Britain.'

* To *shail* means to throw a flat missile, such as a tile, with a gliding motion. The O.E.D. quotes this identical sentence as its earliest illustration.

B

He goes on to give a truly lurid description of the hundreds of loose women who filled the theatres and kept all respectable people away.

'In the theatres it is often difficult to keep off these repulsive beings, especially when they are drunk, which is not seldom the case. . . . And these are the scenes, I repeat, which are exhibited in the national theatre of England [i.e. Drury Lane] where immortal artists like Garrick, Mrs. Siddons, Miss O'Neil, have enraptured the public by their genius, and where such actors as Kean, Kemble and Young still adorn the stage. The turbulent scenes I have described above scarcely ever arise out of anything connected with the performance, but have almost always some source quite foreign to it, and no way relating to the stage.'

This last sentence is significant, for precisely at the epoch when the morals of audiences were at their worst, the censorship was making itself more than usually ridiculous by its pedantry; and the most popular form of entertainment, melodrama, had from its origins been always designed by its French and English authors to inculcate the severest and most virtuous standards of conduct. Macready, on becoming lessee of Drury Lane in October 1841, at once ordered the two circles to be kept free of 'women of the town', but he only brought upon himself the editorial indignation of *John Bull*.

The year 1818 had seen the opening of the Royal Cobourg Theatre, afterwards renamed the Victoria, now officially entitled the Royal Victoria Hall, but better known as the Old Vic. It was run up on the most insecure foundations, as was only too disastrously discovered a century or so later, as a rival to the Surrey, at that time the one theatre south of the Thames. The Cobourg, which had been named in honour of Prince Leopold of Cobourg, consort of the Princess Charlotte, was built on a swamp, but had the advantage of being easily accessible by the new Waterloo Bridge. It was just the moment when the patent theatres were in a chronic state of embarrassment and the minor theatres seemed to be entering on a period of unexpected prosperity. The Cobourg enjoyed royal patronage, and the most eminent actors sometimes condescended to appear there; yet within two years of its opening Hazlitt could give the following description of what took place.

'MARCH 1820. The play was indifferent, but that was nothing. The acting was bad, but that was nothing. The audience was low, but that was nothing. It was the heartless indifference and hearty contempt shown by the performers for their parts, and by the audience for the players and the play, that disgusted us with all of them. Instead of the rude, naked, undisguised expression of curiosity and wonder, of overflowing vanity and unbridled egotism, there was nothing but an exhibition of the most petulant cockneyism and vulgar slang. The genius of St. George's Fields prevailed, and you felt yourself in a bridewell, or a brothel, amongst Jewboys, pickpockets, prostitutes and mountebanks, instead of being in the precincts of Mount Parnassus or in the company of the Muses. The object was not to admire or to excel, but to vilify and degrade everything. The audience did not hiss the actors (that

" — not orange-peel alone "

would have implied a serious disapprobation and something like a disappointed wish to be pleased) but they laughed at, hooted at, nicknamed, pelted them with oranges and witticisms, to show their unruly contempt for them and their art; while the performers, to be even with the audience, evidently slurred their parts, as if ashamed to be thought to take any interest in them, laughed in one another's faces, and that of their friends in the pit, and most effectively marred the process of theatrical illusion by throwing the whole into a most unprincipled burlesque.'

One can imagine a good many people of to-day thoroughly enjoying an occasional scene of this sort, and indeed something nearly resembling it actually did take place in a London theatre only a few years ago. As to what went on at the Cobourg, or at the Victoria, as it was renamed in 1833, there is no lack of contemporary description; the underlying fact, as Mr. Edwin Fagg wisely points out, was that Lambeth had become more closely populated and that the theatre had found its own local audience. It was certainly an audience of the lowest class, and the various managements generally found it profitable to cater for that class. Charles Mathews describes that audience with more genial amusement than Hazlitt. 'The lower orders rush there in mobs, and in shirt-sleeves, applaud frantically, drink ginger-beer, munch apples, crack nuts, call the actors by their Christian names, and throw them orange peel and apples by way of bouquets.' Charles Mathews was the darling of smart society in the days of Lady Blessington and Count D'Orsay, one of the most charming and elegant comedy actors that the English stage has ever known. I think Miss Baylis could have been quite pleased to welcome such an audience in the theatre which she directed, for she often made it plain enough that she did not want the smart people to come inside it at all.

After Victoria came to the throne there was a very general refinement of manners in all ranks of society; it was a refinement which to the present age inevitably appears rather ridiculous – the refinement symbolised by Mendelssohn's *Songs without Words*, the novels of Miss Charlotte M. Yonge, the plays of T. W. Robertson and, a little later, the drawings of George du Maurier. Melodrama continued to hold its own until the arrival of the cinema, which eventually took over all its functions; but to educated playgoers melodrama was rapidly becoming more and more ridiculous unless produced with spectacular effects on the most imposing scale. The Act of 1843 placed all theatres legally on the same level, and it was only natural that a slum theatre like the Victoria should cater for a slum audience. The passing of the Theatre Regulation Act in 1843 was, in the history of the London stage, an event comparable to the signing of Magna Carta in 1215, and consequently of equal importance for the entire British theatre, since the provinces were always dependent mainly on London for the plays which they were to witness. But it is curiously difficult to estimate exactly the effects of the change. For one thing, the Act was not passed all of a sudden; it came as the result of an obstinate struggle protracted over many years, during which more than one change was steadily taking place. The minor theatres, constantly aspiring to rival the houses of privilege, found out more and more ways of evading the letter of the law; the Cobourg and the Surrey were able to mount quite sumptuous productions at times and to attract distinguished audiences, with the result that the patent theatres were obliged to lower their prices and to lower their artistic standards as well. The lower they sank in reputation, the more serious became the social rivalry of the Italian Opera. A distinguished French critic, Augustin Filon, who was no superficial-minded journalist but had a really erudite and scholarly knowledge of the English theatre, remarked in 1896 that what had ruined the theatre in England was the passion for music. To many readers of his book, which was very soon translated into English, this theory must have seemed absurd, for is it not notorious that the English are a totally unmusical nation? Yet seriously I believe that M. Filon put his finger on the right spot and indeed suggested a train of thought that might be pursued a good way beyond what he originally intended to point out. It is certainly true that in those earliest years of Queen Victoria's reign the Italian Opera reached what was probably its highest peak of prosperity; no matter how many managers and syndicates went bankrupt over it, its continuance was steadily maintained and its artistic standards increasingly heightened.

The so-called national theatres resorted more than ever to melodrama and even to the attractions of performing animals, and this during the lifetime of that most austere of theatrical idealists, Macready. Covent Garden became definitely and exclusively an opera house in 1847. The first and most obvious result of the new Act was the establishment of Phelps's Shakespeare company at Sadler's Wells; the next important phase of the new movement was the development of the small theatres with plays of what one might call the 'drawing-room comedy' type, which were peculiarly inviting to the sort of people who came up from the country for the London season and liked no theatres so much as those which filled their entire ground-floor level with stalls to the total exclusion of the vulgarians of the pit.

Outside the theatre it was a great age of social reform, and it is in the serious and often all too humourless world of the social reformers that we first encounter the fairy godmother of the National Theatre, Miss Emma Cons. She came of German stock; her grandfather was a certain Elias Konss who left his native Rhineland and settled in England about 1770. There he changed the spelling of his name to Cons, married, and eventually became the father of a son, Frederick, who was born in 1811. Elias Cons may well have been something of a musician, for Frederick was apprenticed to learn the trade of making pianofortes under the famous firm of John Broadwood & Sons. He married Esther Goodair, the daughter of a cotton-spinner at Stockport, by whom he had two sons and five daughters. The daughters, by some curious oddity of mind on the part of their parents, were all given names beginning with the same letter – Esther, Emma, Ellen, Eliza and Elizabeth.* Elizabeth, generally called by the name of Liebe – one notes how the German tradition persisted in the

* Mrs. Lawrence Haward kindly informs me that this was a traditional practice in thrifty French families; all linen could be marked with the same initials, and each garment, as a child outgrew it, could be passed on to the next.

family – became a singer and married Newton Baylis, a singer too. These were the parents of Lilian Baylis. Emma Cons studied painting, and one of her fellow-students at the art school where she was trained was Octavia Hill, with whom she struck up a friendship. Frederick Cons about this time became a confirmed invalid, and his business began to decline. Octavia Hill's mother had just started the Ladies' Art Guild, to enable gentlewomen to make a living by such artistic abilities as they possessed, and Emma Cons became closely associated with it. In this way she came into contact with Ruskin and other social reformers of the period such as Charles Kingsley and F. D. Maurice. She was earning her own living as a worker in various artistic handicrafts, but gradually she came more and more to share the philanthropic interests of her friend Octavia Hill. Ruskin, being a man of considerable private wealth, bought a London slum property, with the intention of reclaiming it, and appointed these two young women to manage it for him. Emma Cons had already seen a good deal of the life of the poor. She had also worked for Powell's glass factory and had encountered ill-treatment and persecution there from some of the men who were bitterly opposed to the employment of women. This made her a doughty champion of women's rights, and also gave her useful experience in the management of a rough house when she undertook the direction of a theatre.

It was many years, however, before she started, almost accidentally, on the work which has perpetuated her memory. Her business for the present was the collection of rents and the inspection of unsanitary dwellings. But she was intensely interested in the personal lives of the people with whom she was brought into contact, and she soon saw that the most important thing was to keep the men away from the public-house. The reader of to-day may well be inclined to laugh at the apostolic rage with which the social worker of those days pursued the cause of total abstinence. In recent years a certain group of successful poet-journalists (as Osbert Sitwell used to call them) has done its best to make us believe that the public-house – or, as they sometimes prefer to idealise it, 'the English inn' – is the true home of democracy and good-fellowship, frequented by all classes, the clergy included, for the harmless and laudable enjoyments of drinking beer, playing darts and singing folksongs. Have they not indeed historical justification for it? Was not Lucy Lockit (of *The Beggar's Opera*)

'Kiss'd by the Parson, the Squire and the Sot'

while serving her apprenticeship as a barmaid? Those of an older generation can recollect only too well the days when England was said to be the most drunken country in Europe. Not only in the slums of London but in all our great cities and in the country as well one saw drunken people every day, by day as well as by night, women as well as men.* The social workers of those days were only too well justified in regarding the public-house with loathing and horror, and the degradation of the theatre was very largely due to the fact that the proprietors of theatres expected to make their main profits on the sale of intoxicating liquor. Miss Baylis herself says in her memoir of her aunt:

'The public-house, in those days, tempted them [i.e. the poor] at every corner; there was no recreation apart from indulgence in strong drink. With the effects of drink she wrestled daily; and it was the one subject on which this exceptionally broad-minded woman was intolerant.'

With the aid of a few influential people Miss Cons started a series of 'coffee-palaces' to take the place of the familiar 'gin-palaces'. No drinking and no gambling was allowed; men could go there and take their wives with them for a quiet evening. A company was formed to manage these establishments and it was not long before enterprising caterers discovered that there was money to be made out of the temperance movement. The original company came to an end through the competition of the innumerable tea-shops that are familiar to us all, and Miss Cons realised that that chapter of her work was finished. Long before that time, however, she had seen that the poorer classes required not merely tea and coffee but some sort of musical and dramatic entertainment as well.

In 1874 she parted company with Octavia Hill and decided to make Lambeth her chief sphere of operations. It was in this district, at that time one of the most degraded and miserable in London, that she became aware of the habitual association of drink with entertainment. If the men who lived in her tenements came home drunk and assaulted their wives, it was generally because they had been spending the evening at a music-hall where the sale of liquor was a more considerable source of profit to the manager than the price of admission. It may be noted that from the very earliest days the music-hall had grown out of the tavern; Tate Wilkinson tells us that at Sadler's Wells (about 1758) 'a pint of wine or punch was allowed every auditor'. Needless to say this was merely an encouragement to every auditor to order a good deal more wine or punch at his own charge. It is quite possible that Miss Cons's activities in Lambeth, indeed even her determination to settle there, may have been inspired by her friendship with Charles Kingsley, who seems to have known the neighbourhood well, at any rate in his younger days. A passage from his early novel *Alton Locke* has often been quoted as a description of the Old Vic at its worst, and it is worth reprinting here; but it requires a little comment. *Alton Locke*, the supposed autobiography of a young man in the sweated tailoring trade, deals

* It should be remembered that Dickens and George Cruikshank were passionate advocates of temperance.

with the Chartist movement of 1837-48. It was first published in 1850. The hero has been instructed in the aims and principles of the movement by an older workman, Crossthwaite, who takes him one evening to attend a Chartist meeting in Lambeth.

'We were passing by the door of the Victoria Theatre – it was just half-price time – and the beggary and rascality of London were pouring in to their low amusement from the neighbouring gin-palaces and thieves' cellars. A herd of ragged boys, vomiting forth slang, filth and blasphemy, pushed past us, compelling us to take good care of our pockets.'

We must remember that Alton Locke, in the story, had been brought up by a very puritanical mother and, further, that he is a youth with the soul of a poet, who has already started to educate himself as best he can. On this there follows the angry outburst of Crossthwaite:

'Look there! look at the amusements, the training, the civilisation which the Government permits to the children of the people! These licensed pits of darkness, traps of temptation, profligacy and ruin triumphantly yawning night after night! and then tell me that the people who see their children kidnapped into Hell are represented by a Government who licenses such things!

'Give us the Charter and we'll send workmen into Parliament that shall find out whether something better can't be put in the way of the ten thousand boys and girls in London who live by theft and prostitution than the tender mercies of the Victoria – a pretty name! They say the Queen's a good woman, and I don't doubt it; I often wonder if she knows what her precious namesake here is like.'

The Queen in those days was a young mother not much over twenty, and Kingsley himself was the same age as his sovereign. There is nothing exaggerated about the words which he puts into the Chartist's mouth; we can read the same sort of thing in Dickens over and over again, or in the Rev. R. H. Barham's poem about 'the little wulgar boy' in the *Ingoldsby Legends*. The boys and girls who live by theft and prostitution are familiar to us all in *The Beggar's Opera;* there was not much difference between the proletariat of London in 1728 and that of 1848. Crossthwaite's remark about sending workmen into Parliament should be read in conjunction with the report that I have quoted in the preface to this book about a certain political meeting at Loughton in 1929.

Once more Miss Cons called upon her friends in high quarters – this time to get a company formed 'to provide several large music-halls in various parts of London, at

Emma Cons — from a chalk drawing by the late Sir William Rothenstein

which a purified entertainment shall be given and no intoxicant drinks be sold'. Her circular pointed out that at that date there were on an average eight music-halls for every legitimate theatre not only in London but in most of the large provincial towns. This statement is interesting when we compare the situation of the present day, and the proportion not only of music-halls but of cinemas too to the number of normal theatres.

The normal or legitimate theatre, however, was an institution in which Miss Cons does not appear to have taken the slightest interest. 'It is not proposed', says another of her manifestos, 'to provide for a higher class of audience than that which at present frequents music-halls, but only to offer that class an entertainment which shall amuse without degrading them and to which men may take their wives and children without shaming them.' It never occurred to her, apparently, that the inhabitants of Lambeth and other squalid areas might eventually be led to derive enjoyment from ordinary plays; but perhaps her attitude was a perfectly natural one for the age in which she lived. Shakespeare would have been far above the heads of her audiences, drawing-room comedy merely antipathetic to them; melodrama, probably the only form of drama that could possibly appeal to them, was exactly what she wanted to destroy, now that it had in practice ceased to be a drama of lofty moral sentiments and had become mainly a representation of violence and crime.

In any case it was from Octavia Hill that Miss Cons had learned to recognise the value of entertainment for the poor. As soon as Miss Hill had taken over the administration of Ruskin's slum property in 1866 she started a playground for the children and taught them singing-games, even hiring an organ-grinder to provide music for their dancing. Her sister Miranda used to write plays for them. Miss Cons appears to have been curiously indifferent to all this cultural effort. She did not share her friend's enthusiasm for Ruskin and thought little of her desire to beautify the surroundings of her tenants. Miss Hill was naturally distressed at this lack of sympathy. 'It is such a pleasure to me to see things nice,' she wrote, 'and I am sure it has a good influence on everyone concerned. . . . Miss Cons is sure to consider it quite thrown away labour.' The friendship between the two had always been rather tempestuous. Miss Cons was often tactless and insensitive; Miss Hill admired her energy and her enthusiasm, but it became impossible for them to work closely together.

It seems quite clear from the autobiography of John Hollingshead (1895) that he, and not Miss Cons, was really the person who originally conceived the idea of running the Victoria Coffee Tavern as a reformed music-hall. His book is the ultimate source of the manifestoes on the subject which have often been reprinted or quoted, and as he prints these in full himself, we may reasonably suppose that he was to a large extent the author of them. Hollingshead was at that time (1879) one of the most famous and successful theatre managers in London, the creator of the old Gaiety Theatre and of its world-wide reputation as the home of comic opera and burlesque; it speaks well for him that he was at the same time thoroughly sympathetic towards the idea of providing really artistic entertainment for the humblest classes of the people in a district of London that was notorious for crime and depravity. But the Gaiety burlesques of those days were hardly to the taste of the temperance reformers; 'Eventually I found', says Hollingshead, 'that my connection with the Gaiety Theatre was not considered a good and safe qualification for me to take a leading part in carrying out my idea. Being a philosopher, I left it in the capable hands of Miss Cons, and have watched its rise and well-deserved progress with that interest which an abandoned parent takes in the career of a prosperous and proper child.'

— even hiring an organ-grinder —

Miss CONS herself obtained a lease of the Victoria Theatre, which was then in a hopelessly bad way, and opened it on Boxing Day, 1880, as The Royal Victoria Coffee Music Hall. Coffee was eventually discarded as an item in the title, though not at the bar; the theatre still heads its notepaper with the address of the Royal Victoria Hall. For the first few years of its existence the Victoria Hall offered its patrons nothing but an ordinary variety entertainment on most days of the week, except that a careful watch was kept on the proprieties. Once a week there was a concert and on another evening a lecture. The result was a deficit of nearly three thousand pounds on a season of eight months. One can imagine the sort of sound and sensible business men whom Miss Cons had collected around her when one reads that the majority of her council were for closing the hall and sub-letting it, which, of course, would have meant a return to the old system of melodrama and gin, and the complete surrender of all that Miss Cons had been fighting for. Fortunately there were still a few visionaries and idealists who were prepared to stick to her and able somehow to raise the necessary funds for carrying on the enterprise. The Coffee Music Halls Company went into voluntary liquidation; its work was really done, and it could never have established the 'large number of music-halls' all over London which it had envisaged at its inception. Miss Cons formed a new committee, but it was always mainly a committee of philanthropists and social reformers, on which artists or men of letters formed only a small minority. Music, however, was pretty well represented by the names of Arthur Sullivan, Carl Rosa and Julius Benedict; Miss Cons had always kept up her connection with the musical world, and the leading musicians of her day had always been willing to give her their help. But for the moment her most valuable helper was Samuel Morley, a wealthy manufacturer of textiles. He first came into contact with the Victoria Hall in 1884 and he died in 1886, but in those two years his generosity set the place firmly on its feet. By this time Miss Cons had begun to make it something more than a music-hall and a coffee-tavern; it was becoming a place of popular education through scientific lectures given once a week and classes of all kinds for students of the type of Alton Locke. Young people attended lectures for a penny admission and then proceeded to ask Miss Cons for further help and direction in their studies; out of this grew what eventually became Morley College, founded in 1889 in memory of Samuel Morley.

With Morley College this book is not concerned, but it is interesting to note that it grew out of a theatre and that it has always maintained its close connection with the theatre. Its physical connection with the Victoria Hall was for many years nothing more or less than a nuisance and a disastrous obstacle to progress, for Miss Cons had so little idea of what her theatre was going to develop into that she allowed Morley College to occupy dressing-rooms and space both underneath the stage and above it as well, so that when the Old Vic began to be 'the home of Shakespeare', the Bard and his interpreters found themselves hindered and hampered at every turn because half of the theatre was taken up by the ever-increasing activities of popular education. But Morley was eventually turned out and provided with a home in the immediate neighbourhood; and it is gratifying to be able to record that the College is now prominent in the public eye chiefly through its dramatic and musical organisations.

The musical efforts of Miss Cons's management would really be not worth chronicling if it were not that readers of the present day could hardly conceive it possible that such things took place fifty years ago. Once a week there was a ballad concert, and once a fortnight the second half of this consisted of excerpts from an opera sung in costume and accompanied by illustrative tableaux. In these days that section of the musical public which has owed its musical education to Sir Henry Wood and the Promenade Concerts is so much obsessed with orchestral music that it tends to regard any singer as an unwelcome intrusion. But throughout the whole of the nineteenth century purely orchestral concerts hardly existed at all, and even concerts consisting mainly of orchestral items were comparatively rare; what the general public preferred were concerts devoted almost entirely to vocal music, either with some sort of orchestra or with a pianoforte. There would be three or four solo singers, possibly a violinist as well, and an accompanist, in those days often called the 'conductor', who might play an occasional solo. In London, during the last quarter of that century, two rival music-publishing firms organised regular series of what were called 'ballad concerts' and the eminent singers of the day were paid royalties on the subsequent sales of the songs they sang. These concerts were enormously popular, and had a huge commercial value, because in the days before the gramophone and the wireless had been invented (if the present reader can conceive of such a period) amateurs were singing in every drawing-room and the sale of sheet music was far greater than it is now. Schubert, Schumann and Brahms were known only to an inner circle of initiates; Roger Quilter was in his cradle. Even in houses where Mendelssohn and early Beethoven were played the taste in vocal music was all for simplicity. The word *ballad* was no more than a survivor from the days of the eighteenth-century ballad operas; it might mean a genuine British folk-song, or more probably an imitation one; it covered the songs of Bishop and Balfe, of Virginia Gabriel and Maude Valérie White. To the present generation Sullivan's *The Lost Chord* is probably about the only survivor of a prolific spawn amusingly described by Hubert Parry as 'three-verse epitomes of three-volume novels'. These were not the music-hall songs which the bright young people of our own day have sometimes tried to resurrect with the accoutrements of stand-up collars and a false moustache; a sharp line of distinction was drawn between the music-hall and the drawing-room, and the ballad singers were the same as those who interpreted the oratorios of Handel, Mendelssohn and Gounod. Madame Sainton-Dolby, for whom, as Miss Dolby, Mendelssohn had expressly composed *O Rest in the Lord*, was one of Miss Cons's personal friends, and her programmes included most of the 'Madames' of the oratorio platform. All the really famous Victorian oratorio singers called themselves *Madame;* the title gave them an air of dignity and respectability. Nowadays it survives (and the figure also) only in Madame Butterfly.

Among all the oratorio Madames there was none more imposing than Antoinette Sterling (1850-1904), the classical example of what Plunket Greene used to call the 'cavernous contralto'. She was an American by birth and a Quakeress, obsessed by the conviction that her incomparable voice had been specially bestowed upon her by God as an instrument for the conversion of sinners. Her personal sense of a religious mission, which was an integral part of her character, no doubt warmly commended her to Miss Cons and at the same time made her only too willing to support Miss Cons's enterprise. There was something of Mrs. Siddons about her aquiline profile and her grand tragic manner; like Mrs. Siddons too, she was inclined to converse in private life with the thunderous dignity of an ancient Hebrew prophetess. The superb quality of her low notes was unsurpassed even by Clara Butt; her intensity of declamation expressed the austere earnestness of her temperament. To have heard her sing and to have heard her speak was an experience never to be forgotten. When she first went to sing for Miss Cons at the Vic she was unpleasantly surprised to find that the audience smoked, and she told Miss Cons that if the audience continued to smoke she was not going to sing. Miss Cons said she could do nothing; the audience were a rough crowd and would stand no such interference with their pleasures. Considering the habitual courage of Miss Cons in dealing with roughs this moment of timidity seems hardly characteristic of her. Antoinette Sterling had no such terrors. She went on to the platform and said to the audience in that commanding yet homely voice of hers, which never, even after long years of residence in London, lost its endearing American accent, 'I want to sing to you, but if I do, all this smoke will hurt my voice. Now, if you like your pipes more than my singing, why, you go on smoking.' Every pipe was knocked out.

The tableau performances of opera – would they now be called 'tabloid operas?' – were necessitated by the terms of Miss Cons's licence. She explained the situation to her audience in a characteristically worded notice which is worth reprinting here in full, as it shows a delightful petulance and a resolute determination not to put up with the restrictions of a law which stood in urgent need of repeal.

'The management request the kind indulgence of the audience during the unavoidable pauses, which they will endeavour to make as short as possible, but the artistes (*sic*) require time between the songs and tableaux to get behind the scenes and group themselves. Some of the tableaux also require considerable change of dress and scenery.

'The great difficulties with which the management of this Hall has to contend, owing to the unsatisfactory state of the law as affecting Music Halls, may not be generally known to the public.

'By this law they are forbidden *to act* (while holding a Music Hall Licence) even *one* entire scene from an Opera. Were they to take out a Dramatic Licence, they would be obliged by the law to at once stop all smoking on the part of the audience. By simply having Selections from the music of the Opera, sung before a conventional background and illustrating the story by Tableaux, the Management are able to give their audience some idea of the principal Operas without exceeding the limits of their Licence.

'It is hoped that, before long, the law affecting these matters will be revised, and that those who are trying to improve the quality of the entertainment offered to the people will then be less hampered by vexatious restrictions than they at present are.'

Miss Cons, it will be observed, was like many other 'managements' in being unable to make up her mind whether a management was singular or plural. This is the way in which *Il Trovatore* was presented.

Introduction . . . . By THE BAND
Tableau 1. Ferrando arousing the Guard
Duet . . . . 'Oh! Say, Why Stay You'
MISS VAN DALLE & MDME. HENDERSON

(Words follow, but without any indication of which lines are sung by which characters in the duet; the same principle is followed in subsequent trios. Evidently nothing was allowed to be printed which suggested a play.)

Tableau 2. Leonora and Inez in the garden
Tableau 3. Leonora mistaking the Count for Manrico

The operas were all reduced to about twenty musical excerpts and as many tableaux. During that particular winter (1891-92) – the only one of which any record has been preserved – there were fifteen such performances of nine operas: *The*

Bohemian Girl, Fra Diavolo, The Rose of Castile, Maritana, La Sonnambula, Il Trovatore, Faust, The Lily of Killarney and *The Daughter of the Regiment*. The conductor in those days was Mr. Alfred Dove, and the accompanist at the pianoforte Mr. J. H. Maunder, composer of the favourite devotional cantata *Penitence, Pardon and Peace*. The oratorio Madames, it need hardly be said, took no part in these profane diversions.

Miss Cons soon began to find the work of management too much for her and engaged a Mr. Bullock for that purpose, but he did not stay long. He was succeeded in 1881 by William Poel, a son of Dr. William Pole, F.R.S., a very eminent scientist and musical researcher of his time. William Poel eventually became a historic figure in the English theatre, for it was he who started the 'Elizabethan Theatre' movement for acting all Shakespeare, regardless of supposed period, in the costumes of Shakespeare's own day and without scenery of any kind. This idea had been anticipated in 1844 by Benjamin Webster, who tried the experiment of producing *The Taming of the Shrew* after this fashion and was made fun of in *Punch* for it, as one might expect; but Webster does not seem to have pursued the method any further. William Poel began these productions in 1880, but if he thought that he would be able to carry out his schemes under the ægis of Miss Cons he was sadly mistaken. He remained with her for two years and left her in 1883 to become stage-manager to F. R. Benson. Nothing has been recorded of Miss Cons's dealings with her managers in these early years, but it may be guessed that she had her own quite definite ideas of what she wanted to do and that she flatly refused to be exploited or utilised for the benefit of other individuals, even when they were as sincerely idealistic as William Poel. The management of the Victoria Hall must be kept in the family. Miss Ellen Cons, her sister, was already a member of the Board of Governors and continued to be a Governor after the foundress's death in 1912; the only possible person to be entrusted with the task was their niece Lilian Baylis, at that moment living in South Africa.

Lilian Baylis was the daughter of Newton Baylis, a singer who had married the youngest of the Cons sisters. She had been trained in music from her earliest years; she learned the violin under John Tiplady Carrodus, the finest English violinist of mid-Victorian days, and appeared herself in public as a child prodigy. At the age of seven she had helped her aunt with the entertainment of her tenants, and her close association with Miss Cons brought her into frequent contact with the work of the Victoria Hall. In 1890, when Lilian was sixteen, her parents emigrated to South Africa, where they toured a country then as yet only sparsely developed, giving musical and dramatic performances under every conceivable difficulty of transport. Eventually Lilian settled in Johannesburg, where she taught music, organised a ladies' orchestra, and became generally a pioneer of musical education. It was only natural that Miss Cons should wish to avail herself of the services of a young relative already so experienced in the practical side of concert management. She invited her to England on the excuse of convalescence after an operation, and as soon as she arrived persuaded her that it was her duty to sacrifice her lucrative teaching connection in South Africa and devote herself at the meagre salary of a pound a week to managing the business affairs of the Victoria Hall. Sharing as she did the religious convictions of her aunt, she threw herself into the work with unsparing devotion. She became acting manager in 1898, and one of the first things that she did was to engage Charles Corri as musical director in 1889. That musical partnership lasted for over thirty years, and there will be much to be said about Corri in a subsequent chapter.

For the next ten years and more she carried on the affairs of the Hall with a regular routine. No records appear to have been kept of its activities; the earliest existing minute-book of the Governing Body dates from December 1905. On Thursday nights there was music: ballad concerts, operatic tableaux, sometimes an oratorio or a symphony concert. On Saturdays variety shows; the prices of admission for Thursdays and Saturdays were twopence and threepence for the gallery, fourpence and sixpence for the pit, balcony ninepence, stalls one and two shillings. On Tuesdays there was a lecture, for which admission ranged from a penny to a shilling. Friday was Temperance Night and the Hall was placed at the disposal of various temperance societies (there was no shortage of them) for free meetings. On Mondays and Wednesdays the Hall was let for various meetings and entertainments. The Charity Commissioners, under whose authority the Trust of the Victoria Hall was constituted, were resolutely strict in maintaining that the Hall was 'not to be used for any political, denominational or sectarian purposes'. But as long as Miss Cons lived, and for some years after her death, the main policy of the Victoria Hall, as is clearly reflected in the minute-books and in the published annual reports, was primarily temperance and fundamentally religious.

Under the joint influence of Charles Corri and Miss Baylis the practical activities of the Hall tended more and more towards opera and symphony concerts – so much so that the annual report of 1912-14 has on its cover a drawing of the house seen from the stage with the legend 'The Royal Victoria Hall – The People's Opera House'. By 1906 the average attendance at the operas (still given only in tableau form, it must be remembered) was between 1,600 and 2,000. For variety the figure was 1,200, for lectures 750, and for animated pictures 2,000. The cinematograph at that time was in its infancy, but Miss Baylis was one of the first to seize upon it as an attraction. Films in those days were taken from the ordinary events of daily life; just to see a train draw up at a platform and people get out of it and hurry away had all the thrill of novelty. The Guards' Band marched along a street, and to a musical spectator there was something ludicrously incongruous in the sight of drums being

This drawing of a great lady
W. Rothenstein July 1922

Lilian Baylis — from a chalk drawing by the late Sir William Rothenstein

thumped and trombones pulled in and out without the slightest sound proceeding from them. Not even a pianoforte accompanied the films of those days. Miss Baylis noted that the most enthusiastic devotees of 'the pictures' were small children. Within a few years the cinema became a commercial industry; picture palaces sprang up all over London, in Lambeth as well as elsewhere, and Miss Baylis began to find that her takings from 'animated pictures' were decreasing rapidly. For one thing her electrical equipment was primitive and out of date; what was more potent as a counter attraction was that the commercial houses offered films of what she would have called 'sensational' character. The cinema in fact was bringing back to Lambeth and to the world in general the bloodthirsty melodrama of the ancient Cobourg Theatre. Miss Baylis soon dropped the pictures altogether; she was determined that *her* audience, and especially the children, should have nothing but the best.

These early minute-books, as one might imagine, are tedious reading; but one must read them with imagination and try to visualise the people who sat round the table and hear what they actually said. The Board seems to consist mostly of ladies, to begin with; a few gentlemen have sent apologies for their absence, and there is a gentleman in the chair, whose stately signature confirming the minutes of the last meeting tells us all we need to know about his integrity, courtesy and high-minded philanthropic idealism. His name often conveys nothing at all to us; he is the chair-man and that is enough. Miss Cons evidently does most of the talking. She is involved in perpetual struggles against two powers of evil far more tangible than drunkenness or blasphemy, intent upon the destruction of all that to which she has dedicated her life – the London County Council and the Lord Chamberlain. The Lord Chamberlain only bobs up from time to time to worry her about her licence, and when one reads of her negotiations with him, supplemented now and then by the more tactful mediation of Lady Frederick Cavendish behind the scenes, one would think that the Theatre Regulation Act of 1843 had never been passed. The L.C.C. is (to Miss Cons) a chronic nuisance. She had indeed been co-opted a member of that august body herself in 1889, along with Lady Sandhurst and Miss Cobden; they were its first three women members. But from the first it was made clear to them that their co-operation was by no means desired. Lady Sandhurst retired; Miss Cobden and Miss Cons sat firm, but for a whole year recorded no votes. This atmosphere of hostility within the L.C.C. itself no doubt accounts for much of the pugnaciousness, on the part of Miss Cons, recorded in the minute-books of the Victoria Hall. There was a long-drawn battle over protection against fire, a matter on which one would have thought that the L.C.C. had some right to make suggestions. What they did suggest was that Miss Cons should have a telephone installed between the Victoria Hall and the Fire Station; she stoutly refused, on the plea that the nearest fire-station was just across

C

the road. Comparing the accounts of those times with the balance-sheets of to-day, one is struck by the smallness of the sums involved; every detail has to come up before the Board for authorisation even if it amounts to no more than ten pounds or so. Miss Cons and Miss Baylis had to count every halfpenny, and this explains most of that Scrooge-like close-fistedness which in later years seemed to every newcomer the most characteristic quality of Miss Baylis.

Religious matters crop up frequently in the minute-books. A Nonconformist minister, the Reverend D. J. Rouncewell, used to rent the Hall on Sundays for services in connection with his chapel. This was somewhat grudgingly approved 'provided that he complied with the usual terms and conditions, especially as to religious dogma.' What Mr. Rouncewell's doctrinal teaching was is not recorded; but Miss Cons very much resented his desire to make use of her Saturday evening's announcement lantern-slides to advertise his own services. The most influential person on the board was obviously Lady Frederick Cavendish. She was an exceedingly devout High Churchwoman and at the same time a *grande dame* whose social connections were of immense value to the work of the Hall. She was in a position to talk to the Lord Chamberlain privately and even to approach Royalty itself with a request to honour a ballad concert with its presence. Tact and dignity were her principal contributions to the board meetings.

By the beginning of the present century the undertaking had become so firmly settled on its feet that all sorts of other bodies were beginning to think that it might be conveniently utilised for their own purposes. Miss Cons and her committee were unsleepingly on guard against intruders. Oxford House – surely an institution of impeccable respectability – asks to engage the Hall for a boxing competition. Muscular Christianity – was that not in the best traditions of the Reverend Charles Kingsley? Miss Cons grants the application, but cautiously; it is understood that there shall be no disorderly conduct. A request, however, from the National Sunday League to rent the hall for Sunday concerts is turned down with indignation. 'It was decided the secretary be informed the proposal cannot be entertained.' Miss Baylis, acting as Clerk to the Governors, generally prefers concision to syntax.

In November, 1906, William Poel offered to bring his own dramatic company to give performances. What he proposed to perform is not stated; was it *Everyman*, the play with which his memory is inseparably connected, and which later on became one of the Vic's most popular features? In any case the offer was refused, this time with regret, on the simple ground that the Hall was not licensed for stage plays. The state of the law as regards music halls and stage plays has already been indicated in so far as it affected and prevented the complete performance of operas at the Victoria Hall. By 1911 the Lord Chamberlain had been induced to agree to grant a licence to perform stage plays before an audience licensed to smoke at the same time 'provided that no one performance shall contain fewer than six distinct numbers, such numbers to appear on the programme and the Act Drop to be lowered between each item'.

'After discussion' – so the minute-book records – 'it was agreed that this licence was more likely to hinder than to help our opera work.' A reply to the Lord Chamberlain was drafted saying that the Governors had no intention of applying for such a licence since 'their interpretation of the conditions of the necessary undertaking [i.e. the written undertaking for which the Lord Chamberlain stipulated] would, they believe, prevent them from conducting the performances as provided under the terms of the scheme of the Charity Commissioners under which the Hall is worked'. Miss Baylis here achieved what might have been a masterly example of Civil Service English. A year later Lady Frederick Cavendish is still corresponding privately with the Lord Chamberlain. The question arises over a new suggestion that has been made by two young actors employed in Mr. Laurence Irving's company, offering to give Shakespearean recitals. Lady Frederick tactfully suggests that 'it might probably be safe to risk Shakespearean Recitals with our present licence, and not just now to ask the Lord Chamberlain to make an exception in favour of the Victoria Hall'. After some discussion 'it was thought better to adjourn the matter for the present'.

The minute-books indeed show the fundamental wisdom of a policy of masterly inaction, a policy which has for many years guided the fortunes both of the Royal Victoria Hall and of what is now more familiarly known as the Vic-Wells. From this point the demon Lord Chamberlain disappears into the basement of St. James's Palace and the vampire trap ceases to function. He could not pop up through it now even if he would, for no traps have functioned at either the Old Vic or Sadler's Wells since the Dark Ages. Those of the Vic were put out of action by the presence of a safety ceiling to protect Morley College housed beneath the stage, and the traps at Sadler's Wells have been covered over with irremovable linoleum for the exclusive benefit of Miss de Valois and the Ballet. Besides, traps are entirely out of date nowadays; the modern theatre has no use for them. And smoke or no smoke, operas and plays are performed in their entirety.

It was during the course of *Cavalleria Rusticana* that Miss Baylis, who habitually conducted her business affairs from the back of a stage box, reserving her little office behind (when not occupied by leading ladies as a dressing-room) as an oratory for her private devotions, received a visit from the two young gentlemen of Mr. Laurence Irving's company, Mr. W. Bridges Adams and Mr. George Owen, to discuss their project of giving Shakespeare plays in costume on a draped stage with no scenery, calling the performances 'recitals'. One's mind inevitably goes back to 1656 when

D'Avenant produced the first of all English operas under the disguise of 'a moral representation in recitative musick'. In the course of conversation Bridges Adams suddenly observed the tenor on the stage advancing to the apron, casting his eyes apprehensively upwards as the tableau curtains descended behind him. Bridges Adams remembered that the Vic was at that time operating under a music-hall licence, so he understood when Miss Baylis remarked in explanation, 'Breaking the continuity of the Act'. 'What act?' he asked. Wildly and surrealistically (I quote his own words) she replied – one can hear the peculiar snarl of her voice – 'Act of Parliament'. In these ridiculous conditions the Lord Chamberlain expected opera to be performed. Miss Baylis was attracted by the idea of the Shakespeare recitals, but she was taking no risks, especially with a young gentleman who had only just left Oxford. It was agreed by the Governors to let him rent the theatre for six Wednesdays at five guineas a night, but to undertake no further responsibilities; and the Governors expressed the hope that Miss Baylis would not undertake extra work over the matter. Bridges Adams and his friend were unable to raise the necessary guarantee of £100 between them, and the project collapsed.

What is very clear from the minute-books and reports is Miss Baylis's constant preoccupation with the musical activities of the Hall. She and Corri were justly proud of having produced *Tannhäuser* in 1904 and *Lohengrin* in 1906, both, of course, in the inevitable tableau form. Nevertheless, H.R.H. Princess Christian, who was a genuinely keen amateur musician, as befitted a daughter of Queen Victoria, came to a performance of *Tannhäuser* in 1912 and declared herself 'delighted and charmed from the moment of her arrival till her departure'. Let us assume that she arrived punctually and stayed to the end.

In March, 1906, Miss Baylis reported that the Symphony Concerts which had been started by Charles Corri, Exeter Hall very kindly lending music-stands for the purpose, were still financially unsuccessful; but the attendance was steadily increasing and this encouraged the cautious Governors to allow them to be continued to the end of the season. A year later even Miss Baylis felt reluctantly compelled to recommend their discontinuance. Miss Cons never wavered. Hardly a meeting passes without some remark of Miss Cons being recorded, and the reader of to-day might well think these little outbursts merely negligible trivialities, but, taken all together, they bring out vividly her unswerving idealism and her indomitable moral courage. She did not agree with her niece's proposal, and 'called attention to the fact our grant was given us to give good music to the people and raise their taste for same'. The spirit is that of Miss Cons; the grant was that of the City Parochial Fund; the words set down in writing were those of Miss Baylis.

The programmes of the symphony concerts ranged from Suppé to Wagner; they

were certainly no lower in level than some of Sir Henry Wood's Saturday Promenade
concerts. Here is the programme for October 22, 1908: Overture to *Die Meistersinger*
(Wagner), *Welsh Rhapsody* (Edward German), *Italian Symphony* (Mendelssohn),
Overture to *Pique-Dame* (Suppé), Incidental Music to *Henry VIII* (Edward German),
Overture to *Mireille* (Gounod). Other programmes included such things as
Beethoven's *Second Symphony*, Schumann's *Rhenish Symphony*, Brahms's *Tragic Over-
ture*, an *Irish Rhapsody* of Stanford and Sibelius's *Finlandia*, this last a comparatively
new and unknown work.

Miss Cons died in September 1912. She had attended board meetings almost
up to the end, and as long as she lived it was her personality that dominated the
entire policy of the Victoria Hall. It seems appropriate, if not perhaps strictly accurate,
to call the place by that name up to her death and to write of it afterwards by the
name in which it established itself as 'the home of Shakespeare and Opera in English'
– the renewed Old Vic Theatre. From now onwards it was the theatre of Lilian
Baylis, and she proved to be a far more dominating personality than her aunt.
She was equally religious, if not more so, and her religion now became a singularly
conspicuous feature of her management. In the old days she had been merely the
coadjutor of Miss Cons, and Miss Cons was merely one of a considerable group of
social workers whose aims were all quite definitely and openly directed by their
religious principles.

The Vic now became transformed from a temperance hall to a regular theatre.
Theatrical people, and even musicians, may sometimes be profoundly religious in
their private lives, but they do not as a rule parade their religious beliefs in their
professional activities. It would be unjust to accuse Miss Baylis of 'parading' her
religion, but she had no reticence about it and it was always quite publicly exposed.
The result was that in the midst of a very normal crowd of actors and singers it
stood out erect in all its naked sincerity, to some of her family an embarrassment, to
others a source of continuous mirth, and to a certain inner circle a profoundly genuine
inspiration. The word 'family' is deliberately chosen: whoever entered the Vic in any
capacity had to become absorbed into the community whether he wished to do so or
not, and for all those who enjoyed community life there was an extraordinary sense of
what one can only call family affection and family pride. Miss Baylis was a mother to
all of them, though very often like an old hen who has hatched a brood of very
miscellaneous ducklings. For one thing, the 'opera people' and the 'drama people',
united in their allegiance to Miss Baylis, were in practice two worlds apart. Singers
and actors have very different mentalities, and besides that, they worked of necessity
on different days or in different parts of the building, so that they really had very
little chance of ever making friendly contacts. Of the drama side I am myself ill-

equipped to write, and I have to draw mainly on what has already been written by Dame Sybil Thorndike and her brother Russell, by Mr. Harcourt Williams and by Miss Doris Westwood, whose diary of her two years in the Shakespeare company gives a charming picture of the perhaps rather naïve and girlish enthusiasm which permeated a considerable section of that happy community. Only once in those two years did she catch a glimpse of the 'opera people' as she hurried through the back of the circle to a rehearsal in the saloon. 'In the conductor's chair sat an elderly lady, hatless, her arms spread wide, the baton in her hand. And as I watched she rose from her seat, flinging up her arms as if the soul in her were too confined and must burst out on the rush and crash of the music. Now and again she stopped the orchestra, now and again her voice rose clearly as she explained a passage to them, once she sang a bar or two. I was sorry when someone called my name and I had to go to the saloon.' A glimpse and no more. We musicians who came into much closer association with Ethel Smyth became so accustomed to her oddities that we should have found it quite difficult to describe her. For Miss Westwood it was an unforgettable vision, as indeed it ought to have been.

Those who wrote about Miss Baylis during her lifetime were naturally concerned to describe and extol the work which she had accomplished and which she was still actively developing; the writers were whole-hearted admirers and there could be no criticism or belittling of her achievements. When she died – and death came to her much earlier and much more suddenly than it had done to Miss Cons – her more intimate friends, as one would expect, set out to immortalise her and to confer on her an unofficial canonisation. As far as I am competent to judge, the best pen-portrait of her has been drawn by Dame Sybil Thorndike and her brother. One must read the two memoirs together; they are in fact printed in one volume. The reader may choose the viewpoint, feminine or masculine, that the reader may prefer; my own inclination, I confess, is for that of the male memorialist, and I find his description singularly true to life and very sincerely affectionate. But I suspect that stereoscopic truth can be achieved only by combining both angles of vision.

To the outsider she was often grimly forbidding. She had no interests outside the theatre and the church; and the theatre – her own theatre, that is – was a second religion to her, possibly even her first. She was much under the influence of her spiritual director, a clergyman known as 'Father Andrew', whose main work, I believe, lay among fallen women and sufferers from leprosy. He haunted the theatre, and haunted is here indeed the right word, for his tall and sinister-looking figure would sometimes glide silently into the shadows of the Governors' box during a performance, draped in some sort of monastic habit, and suggesting a Grand Inquisitor escaped from the score of some forgotten opera by Mercadante or

Donizetti. I do not remember that I ever had the honour of being introduced to him, but I was told that in private life he was considered to be a man of great kindness of heart. If I myself found Miss Baylis difficult of approach on a first meeting, I certainly was not the only one; recorded utterances of others, and of people pre-eminently distinguished in the world of the theatre, are there to prove it. Ben Greet writes to Sybil Thorndike, 'There's a strange woman running a theatre in the Waterloo Road'. This was in 1914, and it was this letter which led to the Thorndikes' prolonged association with the Old Vic. Granville Barker says to her, 'Queer

Dame Ethel Smyth

Ambrose

woman, Miss Baylis; I don't think she knows anything about these plays, but she's got something'. Perhaps I am tempted to read too much between the lines of the minute-books and suspect all sorts of tactlessnesses behind the all too tactful records. I can only acknowledge frankly that if I found her difficult to get on with, not only at first, but at many subsequent moments, it was my fault and not hers; I had all sorts of prejudices to live down, but a sense of humour generally got the upper hand, and I hope I may count myself as a humble member of 'the family'.

Looking at the Old Vic from the operatic side, I at first formed the opinion that the only hope for a rational development of opera there lay in the removal of Miss Baylis; after a certain time, and after gaining a more intimate acquaintance with its workings, I gradually became converted to the view that whoever else might be recommended for removal, she was the one person whose presence was indispensable. She had been trained as a musician, but I doubt whether her real knowledge of opera was any greater than her knowledge of Shakespeare. She was a pretty shrewd judge of human character and a sound judge of a singer. One day – I forget the year, but it was some time after the opera department was firmly established at

Sadler's Wells – I ran into one of the few really wealthy men of my acquaintance, and perhaps rather too hastily suggested that he should do something to help the opera at Sadler's Wells. 'Why should I help Sadler's Wells?' he asked; 'Sadler's Wells has never done anything for me.' 'What could we have done for you? Have you composed an opera that we might have produced?' 'You've never asked my daughter to sing for you.' I explained that I had no authority myself in the engagement of singers, but I said I would ask Miss Baylis why the young lady had never been offered a part. I did not pass on her reply to the outraged parent. It was brief and to the point. 'She hasn't got any voice.' Miss Baylis always wanted money – that was one of the unpleasant things about her. I asked her once if she had received a letter that I had written to her. 'I don't remember,' she barked out; 'was there a cheque in it?' She wanted money, but she did not want moneyed people inside her theatre. There were boxes in it, and it did not cost much to take one; the Governors' box on the ground floor was an annexe to her private office, and there was another for Royalty, if Royalty happened to come. Otherwise she rather disapproved of people who came to the theatre and took a box – it savoured too much of Covent Garden and social exclusiveness. After her death people wrote about her as 'a great lady'; anything less like a *grande dame* one could not imagine, though she certainly had an ungainly dignity of her own. Her voice was about the most disagreeable that I have ever heard issue from female lips. She might well have described herself – and probably would have done so indeed if it had ever occurred to her – just as Marguerite describes herself to Faust; and like Marguerite, one of her first questions was apt to be that which that young woman addressed to Faust on the subject of his religious beliefs.

Her memorialists, after her death, were not all of them as devoutly reverent as Dame Sybil Thorndike; there was one who was positively malignant in his 'exposure' of her. I have no wish to quote his words, and I did not at the time find them convincing, although on other grounds I should have had every respect for his sincerity and objectivity; and although his memoir is now perhaps better forgotten, I am glad that he wrote as he did, for at that moment it was a wholesome astringent to the gushing adoration poured out by other pens. Miss Baylis was for many people a most difficult person to get on with, but she was undoubtedly a woman of deep fundamental goodness and kindness of heart, in spite of all her ritual adornments, and it was this unshakable goodness of character which made her a peculiarly lovable woman, and the only woman who could hold that entire theatre – those two entire theatres, I ought to say – firmly together, united if for no other cause in personal loyalty to herself. The ugly aspects of her, her close-fistedness and her harsh and almost offensive manner of speaking, were the results of her environment.

In South Africa she must have had to be a
bringer of culture rather than a recipient
of it; in Lambeth she worked among
rough customers and religious enthusiasts.
From the first it was an unending struggle
against poverty and despair; that repel-
lent crust of hardness was a protective
armour that she had either secreted subconsciously or deliberately assumed as a
defence against all sorts of spiritual
enemies. It often seemed to have ossified
all her innate musical sensibilities; during
all the time that I knew her and worked
on the outer fringe of the opera house I
never once heard her say anything about
music which would suggest that she was
a trained musician, or indeed that she
was particularly susceptible to music.

Yet there was no doubt that from first
to last the musical side of the theatre was
what lay nearest to her heart. The whole
thing began with opera, she would often
remind us, and although that did not
prevent us poor opera
people feeling, as we
still do, that opera is
and always has been
the Cinderella of the
family, she herself
was convinced that
Cinderella was the
eldest and the best-be-
loved daughter of her
church. And just as the
youthful promptress of
Shakespeare set down
her passing glimpse of
Ethel Smyth, so let

" — played
the obbligato...from
memory without
a mistake "

me remember our first dress rehearsal of *Don Giovanni* at the Vic in 1921. 'We *must* have a real mandoline for the serenade, Mr. Corri; I can't bear that violin playing it *pizzicato*, even if it is the tradition of all the great opera houses of Europe.' 'Well, ask Miss Baylis; she's the only person here who can play the mandoline.' Considerably surprised, I asked her if she would play it. Still more to my surprise, a mandoline was suddenly produced from nowhere; Miss Baylis hurriedly tuned it, and, what is more, played the *obbligato* to the serenade from memory without a mistake, standing in the wings with the rapt expression of a seraph. She played it for the first performance and no more; she was a little nervous and timid – she had not touched the mandoline for years, she said – so that the instrument was barely audible in the front of the house, and for subsequent performances I am sorry to record that we relapsed once more into the traditional violin *pizzicato*.

IF THE Old Vic became the home of Shakespeare there is no doubt whatever that the first impulse thereto came from Bridges Adams. According to Miss Cicely Hamilton, Miss Baylis used to say that she came to Shakespeare 'by way of the pictures': that is, that when she was unable to find films that she cared to show and that were at the same time attractive to her audience, she turned to Shakespeare as a substitute to fill up her Monday evenings. Miss Hamilton was a close friend of Miss Baylis and I hesitate to doubt her veracity, but I suspect that Miss Baylis's own memory sometimes played her false over minor details. It is clear from Bridges Adams's description that in the winter of 1911-12 the Lord Chamberlain's tiresome restrictions were still in force as regards opera and consequently as regards drama as well. This is confirmed by the minute-book. Nothing more is said about drama in the minute-books until December, 1912, when Miss Baylis reported conversations with Mr. Philip Carr about Shakespearean performances. In January she notes that drama on Wednesdays and Saturdays had been started as at Christmas 'and at present same showed a loss'. It was decided that the performances should be continued. Miss Hamilton says that 'the Governors were more than doubtful about the drawing powers of classic dramatists'. I can well believe it; but as one might expect, they did not think it necessary to record their craven fears in the minutes. Further, Miss Hamilton says that 'the Vic had already adventured into plays – but plays considered safer than Shakespeare; hearty melodramas with no vice in them like *The Shaughraun* – and sketches introduced into the regular variety bill'. There is no mention of these in the minute-book beyond the words that I have quoted above, and nothing about them in the Annual Report. I suspect that the change of policy became possible only after the death of Miss Emma Cons. Her sister Ellen continued to attend board meetings for a long time, but she never seems to have opened her mouth. No further information is available until December, 1913, when Miss Rosina Filippi offered Shakespeare one night a week for four weeks on trial, if the Vic would guarantee her £25 for each night. 'A general discussion ensued. Dr. Scott Lidgett* argued that high-class drama would be carrying out the principles of the work here and should not be lightly refused, if serious loss could be avoided.' The Finance Committee – this is the first time that I find this sub-committee mentioned – were instructed to meet Miss Filippi and discuss terms.

Miss Rosina Filippi had been in her day one of the cleverest actresses on the London stage; at this time she had retired from regular work and was living in

* He is still a Governor of the Old Vic (1945).

Oxford as the wife of a College tutor. She was a popular social figure there and gave valuable help to various dramatic enterprises, notably to the operas conducted by H. P. Allen; she also did a good deal of work as a trainer of young actors and actresses for the professional theatre. It appears from the minutes that the Governing Body on the whole was most desirous of meeting Miss Filippi's proposal, with the exception of Miss Baylis herself, who was against it on the grounds that her audiences were asking for two operas a week instead of one. During February and March of 1914 the Board was still hesitating over Miss Filippi's proposal. What Miss Baylis thought of it privately she did not record. The performances however did take place in April and it was a considerable shock to the Governors that they included not only *The School for Scandal*, but also a play called *Candida* by a Mr. Bernard Shaw. Sheridan could, of course, be regarded as a classic, but the Governors, with a very characteristically Victorian vocabulary, did not consider *Candida* to be at all a 'suitable' play for the Old Vic audiences. In June various newspapers had stated publicly that the Governors objected to Mr. Shaw's play, and there had been press interviews with Miss Filippi, at which that very determined lady no doubt spoke her mind with all the wit and humour that was characteristic of her. The Governors once more wrapped themselves in tact and discretion. 'After some discussion it was decided to write to the above papers stating the fact that the arrangements with Miss Filippi had been for Shakespeare only.'

The next event was the outbreak of war on August 4. The Board met in September and decided to carry on all arrangements as far as possible. In October the National Sunday League once more approached the Governors for the use of the theatre for Sunday concerts. The discussion of this was postponed, and postponed again in November on the excuse of some other engagement to let the theatre on Sundays, but the real reason seems to have been a disagreement within the Board itself. Most of the Governors had by this time come round to a favourable view of the National Sunday League; Miss Cons was no more, but one of her old friends still disapproved. He seems to have carried the meeting with him; the Governing Body continued to let the Hall for religious services on Sundays, feeling on religious grounds that they still preferred services to concerts, although the National Sunday League was prepared to pay twice as much money for rent. One can imagine how high-minded and pleased with themselves the Governors must have felt, and how inwardly distracted poor Miss Baylis must have been, torn between her devotion to piety and her urgent sense of the need for paying court to the Mammon of unrighteousness. A musical Mammon too! But Lambeth in those days had not yet ruled that attendance at a Sunday concert was devotionally equivalent to evening church. The Annual Report for 1914-15 settles the whole matter definitely: Mondays and Wednesdays there are Shakespearean and classical plays, Tuesdays lectures, Thursdays and Saturdays opera in English – and 'on Fridays the Hall can be let for concerts, meetings, etc.' The new reign has begun, and the temperance movement has accomplished its mission; the Vic is the home of Shakespeare. He was pretty badly in need of a home at that moment.

Shakespeare is the symbolic figure of our English historical continuity and the foundation of our spoken language. The history of Shakespearean representation and Shakespearean appreciation is the history of the English theatre and the history of English manners, taste and culture as well. The scholars have grouped his plays in three categories, tragedies, comedies and histories, and as we survey the centuries from 1660 to the present day we can observe how these three categories in practice came to signify respectively the theatre of the actor-manager and the star, the theatre of team-work and ensemble, and the theatre of pageantry and spectacle.

For the Restoration period we must remember that the theatre – that is, the Restoration theatre with its entirely new kind of interior planning, its new Italian scenery, and above all with the novelty of real women as actresses – was a new toy altogether, and that at the same time Shakespeare was definitely 'old-fashioned' – old-fashioned in his theatrical technique and in his language too. If he was to be acted, he must be brought up to date, and no one had the least shame in carrying this out. He survived for the generation of Pepys mainly through the tragedies, which offered star parts for outstanding actors. Pepys's contemptuous criticism on *A Midsummer Night's Dream* is too well known to need quotation, and that play could only be saved by turning it into an opera with music by Purcell.

The operatic treatment of that and other plays of Shakespeare in the seventeenth century belongs really to a later chapter. Restoration comedy, and a good deal of Restoration tragedy too, was created to exhibit the Restoration actress, and when that novelty had worn off, the production of new comedies gradually wilted away. Out of all that was written and staged in the eighteenth century, nothing remains alive now except a handful of comedies by Goldsmith and Sheridan; and yet this was the century of Garrick and Mrs. Siddons, whom not merely English tradition but the united criticism of Europe seems agreed to extol as the greatest actor and actress who ever appeared at any time on any stage. That is where M. Filon points to the possible cause of this incredible decadence of the theatre, the ever-increasing passion of the English for music. It did not begin with Bunn's management of opera at Drury Lane and the first production of *The Bohemian Girl;* it had begun in Shakespeare's own lifetime, if not before his birth; it was preserving the continuity of the theatre during the Commonwealth and either degrading or transfiguring, as the reader may choose for himself, the Shakespeare of the Restoration. And it comes to a sudden head in 1728 with the appearance of *The Beggar's Opera*, the importance of which lies not in its satire, social or musical, but in its immortality. Tate Wilkinson, writing about 1795, expresses his belief (though he owns that he would like to have exact statistics) that *The Beggar's Opera* has been performed more frequently than any piece whatever from the days of Shakespeare. (He means, of course, that it has had more performances than any other play, even including those of Shakespeare.) Note too, that for Tate Wilkinson Shakespeare has by now become 'our immortal bard', our one and only, our national classic; he is no longer what he was for Pepys – a sort of antediluvian Gilbert or Pinero. Pepys never read Shakespeare for his poetry; if he wanted to read poetry, he took *The Siege of Rhodes* out of his pocket. As to *The Beggar's Opera*, it is quite clear from Wilkinson, and from Hazlitt in a later generation, that audiences regarded it primarily as a play and not as an opera, however much they enjoyed the songs. All the same, it is the tunes which have helped to make it a source of familiar quotations like *Hamlet* or *Macbeth*; but it is undoubtedly the play and the play alone which has preserved it – alone out of all the dozens of ballad operas which followed it – down to the present day.

Mrs. Siddons was the sister of John Philip Kemble, and the early nineteenth century is the age of the Kemble tradition, a tradition which must have owed a great deal to that of the French stage, going back to the days of Betterton and Dryden, when the drama was pre-eminently rhetorical, a drama of stately speeches rather than of movement, agitation or violence. And it was, no doubt, that rhetorical tradition which justified Kemble in his incredible mispronunciations of the English language, mispronunciations as deliberately affected as those of Henry Irving. Both actors have been severely censured for them in their own day and both have been defended with equal enthusiasm; in both cases they were perhaps appurtenances of a bygone grandeur, and almost certainly necessitated by the huge size of Drury Lane and the Lyceum, all the more in the days of Kemble, when audiences behaved as described by our German visitor. And even if the Lyceum audience was well-mannered in the last decade of Victoria's reign, Irving had experienced all the brutality and cruelty of an Irish audience at Dublin in 1860. After the Kembles came the flamboyant romanticism of Edmund Kean, another English actor whose name seems to mean more to Continentals than it does to most English people of to-day. His dramatic and indeed tragic end offered an irresistible opportunity to Alexandre Dumas, whose play on the subject of Kean was still popular on both French and German stages in quite recent times. It was the dearest wish of Kean's heart that his son Charles should go to Eton, and with Charles Kean there begins the gradual emergence on our stage of the intellectual, the gentleman actor. It has been constantly debated whether this type has been beneficial to the stage or not.

In Charles Kean's case a classical education infected him with a passion for archæology, all the more since he was himself not a particularly good actor. The great period of stage-pageantry dates from 1824, the year in which Planché designed historically accurate costumes for J. P. Kemble's production of *King John*, to the horror of the noble knights and barons who bitterly resented having to wear what they called stewpans on their heads.

—bitterly resented .... stewpans on their heads

To all these star actors and antiquarian-minded managers Shakespeare was simply indispensable; Shakespeare, and Shakespeare alone, was indeed the only force that kept the British theatre really alive, although what we might call the 'classic repertory' still included Goldsmith, Sheridan, and two plays of a much earlier date, now become museum pieces, Massinger's *A New Way to Pay Old Debts* and Otway's *Venice Preserv'd*. The well-known dictum 'Shakespeare spells ruin' has been attributed to various great actors, but it seems to be rightly traceable to a hack dramatist and translator of operas, James Kenney, and what he really said was 'Shakespeare spells ruin and Byron bankruptcy!' If Shakespeare spelt ruin, in spite of the fact that the public undoubtedly wanted to see the famous actors in Shakespearean parts, it was that the two patent theatres, Drury Lane and Covent Garden, both rebuilt on an enlarged scale after the fires of 1809, were too large to pay expenses. If prices were raised, the audience rioted; and the minor theatres such as the Surrey and the Cobourg were beginning to be serious competitors. The whole aspect of the theatres was being rapidly transformed once more by the almost simultaneous appearance of gas as an illuminant, of a number of new technical devices for the arrangement of scenery and the production of stage illusion, of the new interest in historical research and all branches of archæology stimulated by the novels of Scott (which were immediately dramatised and put on the stage either as plays or as melodramas and operas), and – however much in the background, as perhaps its befitting place – the continuous development of music in the theatre, either as inserted songs and glees or as 'hurries', background music of all sorts and marches to accompany the processions which were now coming to be an indispensable feature of the interminable evening's entertainment.

One of the most significant dates in the history of Shakespearean scholarship was the publication in 1818 – the very year in which the Cobourg Theatre was opened – of 'The Family Shakespeare', edited by Thomas Bowdler, M.D., of Edinburgh, who thereby presented a new verb to the English language. Dr. Bowdler expurgated Shakespeare because he saw that Shakespeare was becoming popular. He could not, of course, be played at the Cobourg as he stood, and not even in Dr. Bowdler's version, but he could be smuggled across to the Surrey side in the disguise of 'a Grand and Terrific Caledonian Drama, founded on Shakespeare's sublime Tragedy of *Macbeth*, interspersed with Characteristic National Marches, Choruses, Combats, and Processions, entitled, *The Fatal Prophecy* or *The Scottish Regicide*'. In 1828 *Hamlet* was converted into 'a New Grand Serious Drama'.

'This piece is not an alteration or adaptation of Shakespeare's admirable Tragedy of the same name, the language, incidents, and, in many respects, the plot being wholly different. It is partly founded on the celebrated French Tragedy by Ducis, and partly on a French Serio Pantomime from the same story. It is confidently hoped that from these materials has been produced a melodrama, possessed of as powerful an interest, and as abundant of striking incidents, impressive situations, and terrific effect, as any that has hitherto appeared.'

Mr. Gordon Craig, in his wonderful study of Irving, quotes Irving's own description of the rough house which he encountered in Dublin in 1860 and says he has seen the same sort of thing himself in Florence. I myself can remember seeing a performance of *Hamlet* in a slum theatre in Rome, acted as a roaring melodrama and

1 Henry VIII, *1933 Season, with Charles Laughton and Flora Robson.* [Photo: Sasha.] **2** The Taming of the Shrew, *1933-34 Season, with Roger Liversey as Petruchio.* [Photo: J. W. Debenham.] **3 and 5** A Midsummer Night's Dream, *1937 Season, with Robert Helpmann and Vivien Leigh.* [Photos: J. W. Debenham.] **4** King John, *1941 Season, with Sybil Thorndike and Abraham Sofaer.* [Photo: Angus McBean.]

1 Measure for Measure, *1937 Season.* [*Photo: J. W. Debenham.*] **2** As You Like It, *1937 Season. Edith Evans and Marie Ney.*
[*Photo: Angus McBean.*] **3** *and* **4** King Lear, *1940 Season, with John Gielgud.* [*Photos: Angus McBean.*] **5** *Laurence Olivier as*
Henry V, *1937.* **6** *Scene from* Henry V, *1937 Season.* [*Photo: J. W. Debenham.*]

1 *and* **3** Hamlet, *1944 Season. Robert Helpmann and Pamela Brown.* [Photos: Edward Mandinian.] **2** *and* **4** Hamlet *in Modern Dress, 1938 Season. Alec Guiness and Hermione Hannen.* [Photos: Angus McBean.] **5** *and* **6** Hamlet, *1937 Season. Laurence Olivier as Hamlet.* [Photos: Angus McBean.]

Hamlet *at Elsinore, 1937.* **1** *Rehearsal.* **2** *Castle at Elsinore.* **3** *Rehearsal.* **4** *During performance.* **5** *The Ghost—Torin Thatcher.* **6** *During performance.* **7** *Hamlet and Ophelia—Laurence Olivier and Vivien Leigh.* [*Photos: London News Agency.*]

heartily appreciated by the audience as such. The modern English reader may perhaps require a note on Ducis, who is not so celebrated now as he was in his own days; J. F. Ducis (1733-1816) did not translate Shakespeare into French, but took some of his plays and rewrote them completely as Shakespeare ought to have constructed them if he had been a Frenchman brought up in the traditions of Corneille, Racine and Voltaire. It was mainly through the versions of Ducis, rather than through other more literal French translations, that Shakespeare first became known in Italy; but he is first mentioned there much earlier by a crazy poet, 'modern' and almost 'romantic', as we might say, who comes into a comedy of Goldoni.

Not only *Macbeth* but various other plays of Shakespeare were transmogrified after this manner at the transpontine houses; the scholarly mind of to-day may be horrified at such desecrations, just as modern musical scholars have been horrified at the contemporary desecrations of Mozart's operas for popular English audiences, but the significance of it all is that the common people wanted Shakespeare and Mozart just as much as the nobility and gentry. In the early 1840's it was worth a manager's while to run seasons of opera in English at the Grecian Saloon in Islington, another of the many theatres of North London which grew out of tea-gardens and taverns.* The passing of the Theatre Regulation Act in 1843 made it possible for a new experiment to be tried in that neighbourhood.

Samuel Phelps and Mrs. Warner took over Sadler's Wells Theatre and reopened it with *Macbeth* on May 27, 1844. Their idea was to establish a permanent company there playing Shakespeare and other standard dramas as well as new plays at popular prices. It was only possible to attempt this in a popular suburban theatre, and to do such things in a suburban theatre was possible only after the passing of the Act of 1843. The first manifesto issued by the new management is worth reprinting here:

'Mrs. Warner and Mr. Phelps embark in the management and performance of Sadler's Wells Theatre in the hope of eventually rendering it what a theatre ought to be – a place for justly representing works of our great dramatic poets. This undertaking commences at a time when the stages which have been exclusively called "National" are closed or devoted to very different objects from that of producing the real drama of England. . . . These circumstances justify the notion that each separate division of our immense metropolis, with its two million of inhabitants, may have its own well-conducted theatre, within a reasonable distance of its patrons.'

From 1844 to 1862 Phelps continued to play Shakespeare at Sadler's Wells; it was from the very first night a thoroughly successful commercial enterprise as well as an

* The Grecian Saloon was formerly the Eagle Tavern commemorated in the popular song *Pop Goes the Weasel*.

D

artistic achievement of the highest educational importance. The *Athenæum*, commenting on the opening, remarks bitterly, 'Society may have outgrown the drama, and by many it is suspected that such is actually the case in England'. The writer notes that Macready, when acting in America, had played to crowded audiences, but not to fashionable ones. 'Here, on the contrary, all classes have long ceased to crowd the theatre to witness the legitimate drama . . . the present time then declares against Shakespeare and legitimate.' Bunn, the critic observes, could only revivify Old Drury with opera and ballet.

It is interesting to read all these criticisms of the early Victorian theatre and to note the attitude taken up by the critics to drama on the one hand and to opera and ballet on the other. Those who read this book will, I expect, think it natural to take an interest of some kind, even if not an equal interest, in all three branches of theatrical art. They may be devout students of Shakespeare, but they will not be likely to make that early Victorian distinction between the 'legitimate' drama and the other kinds of play. This is because a new serious theatre has grown up since the days of Phelps: not merely the polite society comedies of T. W. Robertson, but the drama of a later generation for which the outstanding names are Ibsen and Shaw. The great Victorian writers contributed practically nothing to the stage; their medium, generally speaking, was either poetry for private reading or the novel. The few examples of stage plays written by Browning, Tennyson and Meredith – put on the stage too and given every chance – had as little practical influence on the development of our national drama as those of Byron and Shelley. It would be useless to speak of Sheridan Knowles, Talfourd and Sir Henry Taylor, all regarded in those days as possible successors to Shakespeare; the modern reader has never even heard their names. It was characteristic of those Victorians that they had very little use for music; even if they were susceptible to its charm, like Browning, Thackeray and Meredith, they knew very little about it. It meant for them either the Italian Opera, as something essentially foreign, exotic, idiotic too perhaps, but dazzling and fashionable – morally the symbol of the flaunting ostentation of smart society, or else such music as might be heard in private parlours, the 'simple ballad' of a refined but uncorrupted home life, serving so often both in novel and on the stage too as a background for the repentance of a prodigal son. Our outlook on this musical domesticity has been completely changed by the gramophone and the wireless; as regards the opera, I shall have more to say in a later chapter.

Mr. Barton Baker in his chapter on Phelps at Sadler's Wells evidently bases his account on the same sources, but adds a comment of his own; it is amusing to see how all historians copy from one another and do their best to dish up the old stuff in a new style.

'While our patent theatres were handed over to wild beast shows and were sunk in the deepest slough of degradation, while the fashionable world deserted the drama for the opera, the little remote suburban house – for it was remote in those days from the great centres of London – was nightly filled by an eager and rapt audience, most of them fresh from the workshop, drinking in immortal ideas, of which, but for the stage, they would have lived and died in ignorance.'

If this description of the audience is based on fact and is not a mere figment of the writer's imagination, it shows Sadler's Wells as a remarkable anticipation of what Miss Baylis eventually achieved at the Old Vic.

It would be out of place here to describe the Shakespearean productions of Henry Irving, Beerbohm Tree or even those of Granville Barker, for none of these managers ever put on more than a mere handful of the plays. There was good enough reason for this restriction of repertory. Irving put on the plays in which he himself could take the leading part; Tree was perhaps less of a star actor and more of a general manager, following the example of Charles Kean, but in both cases single plays were put on for long runs with the utmost elaboration of scenic effect. Granville Barker's epoch-making interpretations had hardly begun (1912) when the war of 1914 cut them short; but he too had this in common with Tree and Irving, that elaborate scenery and sumptuous costume were indispensable to the execution of his intellectual idea, so that even if he had been able to carry on his productions he would have had to work on a basis of long runs. Contemporary with Irving was Duke George II of Saxe-Meiningen in Germany, one of the examples of a reigning prince who devoted the better part of his energies to the realm of the theatre. He is the most famous of princely stage-managers, but not the first nor yet the last. King Gustavus III of Sweden wrote opera librettos and designed the choreography of ballets until he was assassinated on the stage of his own opera house in 1792; his tragic end provided a subject for an opera by Scribe and Auber in 1833 which was turned into a romantic melodrama by our prolific and indefatigable Mr. Planché and eventually became the basis for Verdi's *Un Ballo in Maschera*. During the interval between the two wars of our time another German princeling, Henry XLV of Reuss, himself took over the management of his court theatre at Gera; in this case he was the more easily able to undertake opera production as the Revolution had deprived him of his throne. The last remaining vestige of his company survives as 'the Dartington Group,' having found refuge in our own country.

Duke George of Meiningen had not been expected to succeed to the throne, and had, therefore, like our own King Henry VIII, been allowed to develop his own remarkable artistic abilities. He was a singularly accomplished draughtsman in the

style of Moritz von Schwind and others of the German romantic era, as well as an
erudite scholar in the history of art and architecture. When he took command of the
theatre his first object was to do away with the star system and present plays as
organic wholes, especially the plays of Shakespeare. Being also a nephew of our own
Queen Adelaide, who was a princess of Saxe-Meiningen, he had a personal interest
in England and in the monarchical history of England which stimulated him to go
out of his way to secure the utmost topographical accuracy in his scenic settings for
Shakespeare's historical plays. He used to send his artists over to this country to
make drawings on the spot of any palaces and castles which were required for the
scene. Modern Germany has reacted violently against this style and speaks of
'Meiningerei' with contempt, but one could see the influence of the Meiningen
company (which visited England and acted in London) in the meticulous accuracy
of Tree's decorations and also in his brilliantly effective handling of stage crowds,
notably in *Julius Cæsar*, a play which the Meiningen theatre had made peculiarly its
own. After all, if Tree owed much to Meiningen, Meiningen had no doubt been
largely inspired by the doctrines of Charles Kean. It is hardly to be wondered that
Emperor William II had the greatest admiration for Tree and invited him and his
company to Berlin; unfortunately German criticism, on this occasion as on many
others, observed that the imperial taste for English art was at least a generation
behind the times.

All this time scholars both in England and in Germany had been devoting themselves to the textual study of Shakespeare. We take it so much for granted in these
days that Shakespeare will be acted everywhere according to a text which has the
academic authority of Aldis Wright – I purposely name a Shakespeare editor of a
past generation, unrivalled in learning, but now perhaps considered a little out of
date – that we can hardly conceive of the alterations and mutilations made by
D'Avenant, Shadwell, Dryden, Cibber and others which were traditional on the
English stage right into the middle of the last century. When such desecrations were
accepted without protest in the privileged theatres it is not surprising that audiences
across the river were ready to swallow Ducis, or whatever remained of him in
translation and adaptation, provided that they were given processions, combats and
'terrific effects'. The restoration of Shakespeare's own words in the theatre was the
gradual achievement of the intellectuals – Charles Kean, Macready and Phelps.

In the early years of the present century the only place where one could see most,
if not all of the plays of Shakespeare, and where Shakespeare apparently did not spell
ruin, was Stratford-on-Avon, where the Memorial Theatre was tenanted for the
annual festivals by F. R. Benson, whose company was in those days perhaps the most
prolific and inspiring training-school for young actors that existed. Like the Carl

Rosa or the Moody-Manners Company for English opera, the Benson company lived mainly on tour in the provinces, paying only rare visits to London; but wherever it went, it was received with open arms, and few actors or managers can have done more to deepen the conception of Shakespeare as a national possession than F. R. Benson.

All the really great movements in the history of the arts have been brought about, as a general rule, not by the genius of one single inspired visionary, as the public, in its perpetual tendency towards hero-worship, would like to believe, but in the simultaneous impact of more than one causatory force. It was not Miss Baylis alone who built a home for Shakespeare at the Old Vic in 1914; nor would it be true to say that it was only the outbreak of war in that year which made it possible. But the outbreak of war was certainly one of the various impinging forces. It threw the commercial theatre into confusion, for one thing, and that meant that various West End actors and actresses decided that it would be safer to accept an engagement at the Vic on a very small salary but with work guaranteed for eight months than to hang about waiting for the usual type of West End contract, always utterly uncertain whether a play would run for three hundred nights or for barely three. And the Vic offered Shakespeare with a popular audience and a repertory of at least a dozen plays. The Benson company was forced to break up altogether because all its young actors went into the army. Most of those who were still available in the various London theatres had had some experience of Shakespeare; many of them were 'Old Bensonians' with a strong sense of the old comradeship and *esprit de corps*. Nobody knew much about this mysterious Miss Baylis; but Ben Greet and a few others had found that they could get along with her, and gradually the new company was assembled and started work. And there was another force that impinged to make a long and almost exclusively Shakespearean season possible – the reaction against the over-elaborate staging of Tree and Irving. Barker had pointed the way; his productions probably cost him as much as any of those at the Lyceum or His Majesty's, but they looked as if they cost next to nothing. Benjamin Webster as far back as 1844 had tried the experiment of producing *The Taming of the Shrew* in Elizabethan costumes and without scenery; *Punch* had made fun of him with a comic design for *Der Freischütz* in which every item of the complicated Wolf's Glen scene was indicated only by a signboard. But by 1914 every one interested in the theatre had become completely accustomed to William Poel's consistent exploitation of the same principles – all Shakespeare, whatever the imaginary period, represented in the costumes of Shakespeare's lifetime and on a stage without scenery. Miss Baylis always insisted that nothing but the best was fit for her audiences, but whatever that best might be, she was determined to get it cheap – if possible gratis. It was only

under such conditions as these that it was possible for Shakespeare to find a home –
a permanent theatre with a more or less permanent audience of faithful friends, with
intelligent actors and masterly minds to direct them and to frame them in appropriate
but simple settings.

And there was something more than all this, something intangible and difficult
to formulate in words – the subconscious craving for that moral inspiration that perhaps Shakespeare alone of all men could give, the unspoken response to his poetic and
dramatic appeal. The war-propagandists of the last war, and still more those of the
present one, the journalists, the authors of versified advertisements, the makers of
patriotic films, have succeeded between them in making the word 'patriotism' stink
so vilely that one is almost ashamed to write it down. Well did Doctor Johnson
call it the last refuge of a scoundrel. Yet if at the bottom of Pandora's box of horrors
we may sniff the faint aroma of hope, we can turn at least to Shakespeare, not for
the pompous rhodomontades so often quoted
on patriotic occasions but for the eternal beauty
of his language, for the endless procession of
characters and types that have made us regard
him as the symbol of our his-
toric continuity with the spirits
of our ancestors. It is true not
only for the actor on the stage
but for every one of us in the
audience that
somewhere in
Shakespeare we
can always find
the portrait of
our own inward
and ideal self.

Audience at
S' Wells Opera

THE HISTORY of opera in this country is curious and complicated; it is also very characteristically English in its mixture of amateurish enthusiasm, professional indifference, occasional bright ideas without the least sense of planning for the future, commercial routine and – from the general public – complete ignorance and bewilderment. The first creators of opera in Italy were enthusiastic amateurs, too, and in Italy, too, opera eventually became commercialised until in the course of the last three centuries it has been one of Italy's most flourishing export industries, as it is still. But in Italy opera began as an exclusive sort of entertainment for the amusement of courts; it was the expensive plaything of princes who lived in an age when the fashion was all for academic intellectualism. Our social leaders in England copied the masques which had preceded the invention of opera; all the ingenuities of Inigo Jones were borrowed from the entertainments of the court of Florence. But just at the moment when opera in Italy was developing into something more than an academic experiment, our own court and its entertainments had to go into hiding; when Charles II returned to assume the crown he would have been delighted to imitate all the grandeurs of the court of Versailles, if he could have persuaded the nation to pay for them. In other countries opera had begun to be one of the regular appurtenances of monarchy; it was essentially an entertainment for the glorification, rather than for the amusement, of royal and imperial houses. The king of England preferred other diversions; Parliament was concerned with more serious matters, and opera, in so far as it had any existence at all, was pursued only by a few poets and musicians, dependent for its prosperity not on a royal subsidy but on the capricious favour of the public. The first of all English operas, *The Siege of Rhodes* (1656), was what one might call an academic experiment, not for a court function, but for any intellectuals who cared to find their way to the author's private house. The importance of *The Siege of Rhodes* was that it was entirely English and something entirely new, both for English music and for opera in general; it was not a translation from the Italian, and not in the least like any Italian opera of its time, as far as the libretto went – the music has entirely disappeared. All that it led to after the Restoration was the operatic treatment of Shakespeare, the revival of such plays as *The Tempest*, *Macbeth* and *A Midsummer Night's Dream* with an ever-increasing quantity of incidental music, culminating in Purcell's *King Arthur*, planned by Dryden as a 'dynastic' opera on the lines of those in which Lully glorified the magnificence of Louis XIV. William and Mary had no great desire for glorification; Dryden and Purcell, like D'Avenant and his group of composers before them, and like Arne, poet and musician in one, half a century later, did what Englishmen generally do – they arrived on the scene of action after everything was over. The Harrogate audience of 1774 mentioned in a previous chapter was typical of our habitual time-lag in all things musical and artistic.

Charles II had once imported a French opera, sung in French by singers from Paris. The first imported Italian opera with Italian singers seems to have been Greber's *The Loves of Ergasto*, performed at the opening of Vanbrugh's new theatre in the Haymarket (1705), but there is some uncertainty about this. Eight Italian operas were given about this time either at the Haymarket or at Drury Lane, sung in English translations by English singers; these are the first cases of foreign operas translated into English. But the fashion did not last long. Addison's attempt at a real English opera, *Rosamond* (1707), was a ridiculous failure, and in a few years London society had completely succumbed to the charm of Italian singers singing in their own language. The court occasionally patronised the opera, but did not subsidise it. The Italian Opera at the King's Theatre in the Haymarket was carried on by an endless series of committees and syndicates, each going bankrupt after a few years of management. But bankruptcy never seemed to matter; new guarantors always made their appearance and while in other countries Italian opera was paid for out of the monarch's privy purse, except in France, where the Opera remained consistently French, the Italian Opera in London was the entertainment of the nobility and gentry, and its theatre for two hundred years and more the exclusive resort of aristocratic society.

From the date of *Almahide* (1710), generally supposed to be the first opera given entirely in Italian in England, no more foreign operas were translated for half a century. This may seem surprising, but it is not impossible to account for it. In the early part of the century Paris had cultivated a sort of opera called *vaudeville*, in which tunes were taken ready made from all sorts of serious operas by Rameau and others, set to new words, and interspersed in the course of comic plays. It was very much the same sort of thing as *The Beggar's Opera* in England. *The Beggar's Opera* (1728) was followed by a long series of ballad operas which utilised popular tunes, and especially tunes that we should now class as folksongs, but none of them attained the immediate success of *The Beggar's Opera*, nor did any of them achieve its apparent immortality, an immortality which is undoubtedly due to the brilliantly amusing play and not to the music itself, charming as the songs have always been considered. Writers on music often talk of 'ballad opera' as if it went on for another hundred years; but even if operas of the later generation were given this title in print, the system on which they were composed was entirely different. It never seems to have occurred to any English composer except Arne to consider an opera as an organic

whole, a thing to be the musical work of one man; foreign operas were utilised and
their songs adapted to English words, but often to an entirely different story. If on
the other hand the story was translated, the music was altered and new songs by
other composers inserted. As an occasional exception we may mention *The Fairies*
(1755), an adaptation of *A Midsummer Night's Dream* falsely attributed to Garrick,
with music by John Christopher Smith, the son of Handel's old copyist; Horace
Walpole writes of it with utter contempt. Piccinni's *La Buona Figliuola* (Rome, 1769),

Farinelli
Italian singer
sang in London 1737

originally founded on Richardson's *Pamela*, was given in London in Italian in
November, 1766; in the following month it appeared in an English translation, and
the translator claimed that this was 'the first attempt of bringing an entire musical
composition on the English stage'. This was printed in London as *The Accomplish'd
Maid;* but only a few years later the opera was revived in English in another translation with music by Michael Arne. In nearly all these English comic operas the music
was a mixture of all sorts of songs from foreign operas, with perhaps some ensembles
by the English composer who strung the whole together.

When we consider this half-century of *pasticcio* or patchwork opera in England,
it need not surprise us to find that the operas of Mozart and Rossini were treated in

exactly the same way. Even at the Italian Opera they were not always given according to the composer's score; numbers were left out and additional music by other composers freely inserted to suit the singers. In the English performances conducted by Bishop alterations were necessitated because the popular English actors could not sing at all. We must not be too severe on Bishop; he was doing very much the same thing as Charles Corri was doing a hundred years later at the Old Vic. He wanted to give the common people as much as they could be persuaded to swallow of the masterpieces of opera which up till then had been accessible only to the fashionable and wealthy audiences of the Italian Opera House. Augustin Filon seems to have said no more than the truth when he observed that the English theatre was ruined by the passion for music. He noted that first in 1840, but it really dates back to the Restoration. Not only was it necessary to turn Shakespeare's plays into quasi-operas; there is hardly a play of any kind, comedy or tragedy, in Restoration days without at least one song inserted, generally sung by a singer who walks on for the purpose, not by one of the chief characters. In the reign of Queen Anne the Italian opera begins to be a permanent counter-attraction for the wealthy, and the innumerable ballad operas, comic operas, romantic operas and musical pieces in general the delight of more popular audiences. Things were no better in the days of the Kembles than in those of Betterton; to a student of English operatic history noting the gradual progress towards real English opera there is something very amusing about the indignation of Professor Odell and others over the 'operatisation' of Shakespeare. The general public, then as always, had no very clear idea what it wanted; indeed, that inability to make up its mind has been the bane of our theatre all along, for even now it is utterly impossible to forecast what will be a success on the stage. Generally speaking, the public wants outstanding personalities, individuals who can really do something or other, whatever that something may be. It adores the singer, but does not understand that it is the song which makes him a singer. Another thing that the public adores is spectacle, and similarly it does not realise that the musical background is half the spectacle, for it throws the audience into an emotional state that prevents them from noticing how inadequately the spectacle is really presented. The function of music in the theatre has been all along the same as it has been in the circus, in the cinema (especially in the old-fashioned silent cinema) and in the restaurant where it distracts attention from the badness of the food and the stupidity of our neighbour's conversation.

The melodrama, imported from France at the end of the eighteenth century, was practically an opera without music: that is, it was constructed very much on the lines of an opera, with its long soliloquies and its *buffo* scenes, but spoken and not sung, as well as its choruses which were sung, as in the old Purcellian operas, and its descriptive instrumental music. Another characteristic of the melodrama was the 'tableau' at the end of an act and sometimes in the middle of a scene. Sheridan parodies it in *The Critic;* it was derived from the operatic finale and the operatic ensemble that had recently become the fashion. There was no very clear distinction between melodrama and opera itself. Weber's *Der Freischütz* came out at Berlin in 1821; but be it noted that it was produced in the royal playhouse, not in the royal opera house. Washington Irving saw it in Germany in 1823 and began to make a

translation for the London stage; it is evident that he had not the remotest conception that he had been listening to one of the great masterpieces of German music. He saw it as a melodrama, not a very good one really, but still one that might be made something of if the story was considerably pulled about and re-written. As to the music, some of the songs were quite pretty; the casting of the magic bullets presented great opportunities for spectacular effects, and, of course, any sort of music would do as a background for that. In 1824 there were no less than six separate productions of *Der Freischütz* in London. Hitherto historians, including that most recent and most accurate of researchers Dr. Loewenberg, have regarded that of the Lyceum (July) as the first. In August it came out as an equestrian melodrama at Astley's, in September at the Surrey, adapted by Fitzball, in October at Covent

Garden, adapted by Planché and Barham Livius, and in December at Drury Lane with additional music by Bishop. But there was an earlier performance still. Miss Cicely Hamilton in her history of the Old Vic reproduces a playbill of the Cobourg dated February 26, 1824, on which the third item is 'an entirely new Legendary Melodrama, called *The Fatal Marksman or the Demon of the Black Forest*'. There is no mention of Weber; 'the new music' was by Mr. T. Hughes, a composer whose works I have sought in vain in the British Museum catalogues. From the list of characters, the synopsis of scenery and other descriptive matter, it is quite evident that this is a free adaptation of the opera, or perhaps more accurately, an adaptation from the original German story on which the opera is based, but with some indebtedness to the opera libretto. We may take it as quite certain that the story would never have reached the English stage unless it had already been made famous in Germany by the enormously successful music of Weber. Even in the five other productions very little of Weber's music was allowed to survive. The Cobourg's version – I have been unable to trace the libretto in the British Museum, although the melodrama is listed by Allardyce Nicoll from the Lord Chamberlain's records – is peculiar in that among the minor characters it includes 'Molly Mug, a Military Spinster', acted by Mr. Sloman. She does not come into Weber's opera.

Prince Pückler-Muskau, as one might expect, has plenty to tell us about the operatic activities of London, and here he is more or less on his own ground. Let us first go with him to the King's Theatre in the Haymarket. The opera is Rossini's *La Cenerentola*, an opera then just twelve years old, and Malibran sings the title-part. 'She has married an American, and her style of singing appeared to me quite American – that is, free, daring and republican.' Of the house itself he says:

'Here you find the most select audience: it is the fashionable house. The theatre is prettily decorated, the lighting brilliant, and the singing exceeds expectation. Still it is curious that even with a company composed entirely of Italians the singing is never the same – there is never that complete and inimitable whole, which you find in Italy; their fire seems chilled in these colder regions, their humour dried up; they know that they shall be applauded, but that they no longer form one family with the audience; the *buffo*, as well as the first tragic singer, feels that he is but half understood, and, even musically speaking, but half felt. In Italy the opera is nature, necessity; in Germany, England and France, an enjoyment of art, or a way of killing time.'

A few months later he was at the English Opera, evidently the theatre which eventually became the Lyceum.

'The house is neither large nor elegant, but the actors very good. There was no opera, however, but hideous melodrama; first *Frankenstein*, where a human being is made by magic – a manufacture which answers very ill; and then *The Vampire*, after the well-known tale falsely attributed to Lord Byron. The principal part in both was acted by Mr. Cooke, who is distinguished for a very handsome person, skilful acting and a remarkably dignified, noble deportment. The acting was indeed admirable throughout, but the pieces so stupid and monstrous that it was impossible to sit out the performance. The heat, the exhalations and the audience were not the most agreeable.'

In view of the modern cult of Mozart, two descriptions of early English performances may be of interest. The first shall be from Hazlitt. *Don Giovanni* was first performed in London in Italian at the King's Theatre in April 1817; it had twenty-three performances. Six weeks later Covent Garden staged it in English as *The Libertine*, translated (?) by Isaac Pocock, the music adapted by Bishop. Hazlitt saw both productions; he was evidently a devoted enthusiast for Mozart, though he scoffs at the current talk about the 'sublimity and Shakespearean character of Don Juan'. What he saw at Covent Garden he calls 'an after-piece altered from Shadwell, with Mozart's music'. Charles Kemble was the Don, but as he was no singer, his part in *Là ci darem la mano* had to be given to Masetto (Mr. Duruset). Miss Stephens as Zerlina did sing the original songs.

'Indeed, all the performers seemed, instead of going their lengths on this occasion, to be upon their good behaviour, and instead of entering into their parts, to be thinking of the comparison between themselves and the performers at the Opera. We cannot say it was in their favour.'

Our German Prince, nine years later, goes to see *Figaro* at Drury Lane. The first Italian performance had been in 1812; the first in English at Covent Garden in 1819.

'You will hardly believe me when I tell you that neither the Count, the Countess nor Figaro sang; these parts were given to mere actors, and their principal songs, with some little alteration in the words, were sung by the other singers; to add to this, the gardener roared out some interpolated popular English songs, which suited Mozart just as a pitch-plaster would suit the face of the Venus de' Medici. The whole opera was, moreover, "arranged" by a certain Mr. Bishop (a circumstance which I had seen noticed in the bill, but did not understand till now) – that is, adapted to English ears by means of the most tasteless and shocking alterations.
'The English national music, the coarse heavy melodies of which can never be

mistaken for an instant, has, to me at least, something singularly offensive; an expression of brutal feeling both in pain and pleasure, which smacks of "roast-beef, plum-pudding and porter". You may imagine, therefore, what an agreeable effect these incorporations into the lovely and refined conceptions of Mozart must produce.

'This abominable practice is the more inexcusable, since here is really no want of meritorious singers, male and female; and with better arrangement, very good performances might be given. It is true, even if the stage were in good order, a second Orpheus would still be required to tame English audiences.'

— a second Orpheus —

The production of Weber's *Oberon* in London (1826) was a notable landmark in our operatic history, for here was an entirely new opera composed all through (though by no means what the Germans would call *durchkomponiert!*) by one composer, and that a very distinguished one, to English words and commissioned by an English manager; it was not a *pasticcio*, not a translation, nor an adaptation. But the librettist, Planché, admitted frankly that *Oberon* was not really an opera but a melodrama with songs.

'Had I constructed it in the form most agreeable to me and acceptable to Weber, it could not have been performed by the company at Covent Garden, and if attempted must have proved a complete fiasco. None of our actors could sing, and but one singer could act – Madame Vestris, who made a charming Fatima.'

The success of *Oberon*, however, paved the way for more complete translations of foreign operas, and finally for complete operas by English composers. This phase of English opera more or less covers the reign of William IV. With the accession of Victoria and her marriage to an intensely musical Prince a considerable impulse was given to English opera. Queen Adelaide had shown some interest in music, for she was a princess of Saxe-Meiningen and aunt of the theatrically-minded Duke; Victoria, however, seems to have been the first English sovereign who ever attended an English opera – Balfe's *Siege of Rochelle*; Fitzball mentions the fact in his memoirs – 'the first time Her present Gracious Majesty went in state to the theatre, it was to the Theatre Royal, Drury Lane, *The Siege of Rochelle* being performed by *special desire*'. This was probably in 1837; Balfe's opera was first produced in 1835.

John Hollingshead gave a pleasant account of opera in English at the Grecian Saloon in City Road, Islington, where a Mr. Rouse ran what Hollingshead compares to the beer-garden of some little unsophisticated German town, with tobacco and moderate stimulants, music and drama at cheap prices. The price of seats ranged between sixpence and two shillings. Smoking was allowed anywhere. The opera repertory was mostly taken from French *opéra-comique* – Auber being as always the most popular composer; but Rouse also performed *The Barber of Seville*, *La Gazza Ladra*, *La Sonnambula*, *Der Freischütz*, and Barnett's *Mountain Sylph*.

Towards the middle of the century there were very successful seasons of opera in English under the management of Louisa Pyne and William Harrison. This was the age of Balfe and Wallace; *The Bohemian Girl* came out in 1843,

"*— an intensely musical prince*" with Queen Victoria leads the waltz.

Maritana in 1845, and these were only among the earliest of a long series of operas by native composers some of which might well be revived again. Hollingshead introduced opera in English at the Gaiety from 1870 onwards, again mostly with French *opéra-comique* as his mainstay. It is only natural to suppose that his success with opera of this type encouraged him towards the idea of opening the Victoria as a popular opera-house.

After the period of Hollingshead came two separate and almost simultaneous operatic enterprises, the Carl Rosa company founded in 1875 and the Gilbert and Sullivan operettas beginning with *Trial by Jury* in the same year. All this time, it should be remembered, the Italian opera was continuing under various managements either at Her Majesty's or at Covent Garden or at both. From this date begins the gradual growth of a curious tendency among audiences to divide opera into two categories, 'grand opera' and 'light opera', thereby perpetuating many misconceptions and misunderstandings. Many people might imagine that 'grand' and 'light' opera were only the modern descendants of *opera seria* and *opera buffa* in the eighteenth century; some might even point to Paris and say that it was only the logical distinction of the French mind between *grand opéra* and *opéra-comique;* a few might even seek to maintain that the two categories stood really for tragedy and comedy. It is curious, by the way, that whereas 'musical comedy' now signifies a quite definable *genre*, the antithesis 'musical tragedy' is absolutely unknown, at any rate in the English language. It is obvious that the use of the ridiculous word *grand* in musical connections has come from the French; Grove in the first edition of his Dictionary (1879) considered that it was in those days happily becoming obsolete. It is true that we no longer advertise a 'grand symphony' or 'grand concerto', still less a 'grand trio' such as is now remembered only by that of Hummel so rashly attempted by the famous South American lady. We still speak of a 'grand pianoforte', but 'grand' opera is really an utter misnomer. The technical French distinction is between opera in which the music is continuous all through and that in which the musical numbers are interspersed with spoken dialogue. To this definition the subject or character of the plot and its treatment are irrelevant. *Carmen, Fidelio, Freischütz,* all belong to the class of *opéra-comique* and would still be inadmissible at the great opera house in Paris unless they were provided with sung recitatives.

English romantic opera, as exemplified in *Maritana*, grew not out of *opera seria* or *tragédie-lyrique*, but out of French *opéra-comique*. It was French inasmuch as it was an obvious imitation of the Scribe-Auber type, and even when it seemed to throw back to the traditions of the ballad operas of our own country its construction was based on the operas of Sedaine and Monsigny. It might be as romantic as Bunn or Fitzball could make it, but it always preserved its separate numbers, its spoken

1 *Scene from* Madame Butterfly, *1942 Season.* [*Photo: Angus McBean.*] **2** *Laurance Collingwood, Conductor.* **3** *Scene from* La Bohème, *1936 Season.* [*Photo: J. W. Debenham.*] **4** *Scene from* The Barber of Seville, *1940 Season.* [*Photo: J. W. Debenham.*] **5** *Scene from* The Travelling Companion, *1935 Season.* [*Photo: J. W. Debenham.*] **6** *Scene from* Cosi fan Tutti, *1944 Season.* [*Photo: Alexander Bender.*] **7** *Scene from* I Pagliacci, *1937-38 Season.* [*Photo: J. W. Debenham.*]

1 *Coronation Scene from* Boris Godounov, *1937 Season.* **2** *Scene from* Marriage of Figaro, *1936 Season.* **3** *Scene from* Don Giovanni, *1937 Season.* **4** *Scene from* Fidelio, *1937 Season.* **5** *Scene from* Die Meistersinger, *1936-37 Season.* **6** *Scene from* The Magic Flute, *1936-37 Season.* **7** *Scene from* Aida, *1937-38 Season.* [*Photos: J. W. Debenham.*]

dialogue and its comic characters. English composers experimented a good deal with recitative in the seventeenth century, and Purcell indeed achieved a musical declamation unsurpassed by J. S. Bach or even by Rameau; but from the beginning of the eighteenth century onwards one could cite dozens of writers who maintain firmly that the English theatre has no use for it. It was just the same in France and Germany; recitative might be tolerated for short passages in the grand rhetorical manner of Gluck, accompanied by the orchestra, but for getting over the ground quickly, spoken dialogue was always the most practical thing. The Italians, on the other hand, always stuck to recitative, and accompanied it with the harpsichord whether the literary content was comic or serious. Common sense tells us that in comic passages or, indeed, wherever naturalism was required, the Italian singers must have approximated very closely to speech, and did not treat their recitatives in the style considered traditional for Handelian oratorios in the Albert Hall. In German theatres the comic operas of Mozart and Rossini were always given with spoken dialogue, when performed in German, from their first productions well on into the last century. By that time, alas, they had ceased to be comic; they were classics to be reverenced, or else grand operas in which elderly celebrities showed off their voices. The damage was done in Paris and London in the glorious days of Grisi, Mario and Lablache – roughly speaking, between 1840 and 1860. Italy was more impoverished than ever, its population at that moment more interested in politics than in music; Italian opera was an export industry, and the best Italian opera performances were to be seen in Paris and London. The national French Opera continued its activities, but it was the *Théâtre des Italiens* where the most fashionable society was to be found. It was the most expensive theatre in Paris, much more expensive than the national Opera House. London drew on Paris for most of its Italian singers. The consequence was that operas such as Mozart's *Figaro* and Rossini's *Barber*, intended originally for small and intimate houses, were forced into the same category, by stress of environment, as the spectacular operas of Meyerbeer and the noisy melodramas of the early Verdi. All operas had to be given in Italian, and so all had to be provided with recitatives, *Carmen* and *Fidelio* included, when their time of popularity arrived.

The Carl Rosa company, working in rivalry with the Italian Opera, naturally aimed at the grand manner, all the more so as Rosa, being a German violinist, showed a natural inclination towards the symphonic outlook in opera; it was just the moment when Wagner began to make his influence felt even in this country. In the other direction Auber led quite easily into Offenbach, Hervé, Lecocq and Planquette, from which the transition to Sullivan was the next step. Sullivan was a conscientious artist with serious ambitions to be something more than an English Offenbach; but he was at the mercy of his public, and his successors – after Edward German we

E

need not name them – pursued paths which led to theatres more lucrative than Sadler's Wells, perhaps even more lucrative than the Savoy.

The fatal result of this misunderstanding, this stupid division of opera into two categories, 'grand' and 'light', has been that a large section of the public still hankers after what it imagines to be the glories of old Covent Garden, and would rather hear fat and elderly singers screaming and bawling their way through Mascagni and Puccini than see the young and intelligent in clever ensemble productions (but with

spoken dialogue) of *Figaro* and the *Barber*. Perhaps they think they are not getting their money's worth unless the singers are singing all the time. What really embarrasses them, I think, is that as soon as singers begin to speak, they are aware of them as real human beings and aware of the absurdity of a Rosina who is nearer sixty than sixteen.

Charles Corri at the Old Vic proved that there was really a public, and a popular public, for opera in English. Even now there are eminent critics still living who

Barber of
Seville

firmly and quite seriously maintain that the only right and proper way to put grand opera on the stage is for the solo singers to come down to the footlights and for the chorus to stand still in two rows. If that principle be accepted it is almost surprising that Miss Baylis should have resented the Lord Chamberlain's restrictions, for the difference between tableau opera and grand opera seems hardly perceptible. Miss Baylis had been brought up in the old conventions and she found them convenient as well, for they allowed her to present opera with the absolute minimum of rehearsal. The only way in which she could get her singers cheap was by demanding as little as possible from them. If they were not required to rehearse they had all the more time free for other engagements, and it was characteristic of Miss Baylis's innate goodness of heart that she was always ready to endanger her own artistic standards rather than stand in the way of a singer's or dancer's private welfare. In the ideal opera house the singers are always at the disposal of the management for rehearsals as well as for performance, but if that is expected from them they have to be paid accordingly. That was naturally quite beyond the means of the Old Vic. The chorus were volunteers, at work elsewhere during the daytime; they could only attend rehearsals on occasional evenings, so no very serious artistic burdens could be thrown upon them. New singers who appeared for the first time were often pitchforked on to the stage without any rehearsal at all, even in an opera which they had never sung before. They were given a few hasty directions by the stage-manager 'and someone in the chorus 'll tell you what you do next'.

Needless to say the expenses of the orchestra had to be kept down to the barest necessities. Eighteen or nineteen players was the general rule – single wood-wind, two horns and strings; sometimes perhaps a trumpet and kettle-drums, and if Wagner was being acted, one trombone and two more horns. A small pianoforte functioned as a harp. Corri showed himself a truly accomplished artist. He would have scorned the usual methods of the minor touring companies in which the conductor plays what he can on the pianoforte with his left hand while conducting with his right, the band getting along as best they can with standard parts and perhaps a few missing instruments cued in here and there. Corri devoted his summer holidays to the laborious task (yet I will not believe that it was a tedious one) of completely reorchestrating the standard operas for this small assembly, not just cutting out instruments anyhow, but using a composer's imagination to think out how Mozart or Wagner would have scored the operas had they been faced with a small band like this from the very start. The result was that Corri's orchestra at the Vic was always satisfactory and in a way adequate, adequate, that is, for its environment. Whatever effects the learned connoisseur might miss (and fortunately the learned connoisseurs – if they *are* learned, which I very much doubt – did not frequent the Old Vic), the orchestra always had a proper consistency and balance of tone, and what was still more important, it never overpowered the singers, for whom Corri showed a good deal more consideration than most of the celebrated conductors.

Another fine artist of the Vic in those days was Sam Harrison, for many years stage manager. His daytime occupation was selling gramophones, I believe. He was of short stature and not very imposing appearance, and habitually spoke with a strong north-country accent; his usual rôle in opera was the *père noble*. My first sight of him, as far as I remember, was in *Mignon;* he sang and acted the venerable harpist Lothario with astonishing dignity and pathos. He was incredibly funny as Masetto

"Of course I suppose those wretched singers have to be terribly careful what they wear"

in *Don Giovanni*, all the funnier for playing the part with a stronger Manchester accent than ever, and a distinct touch of the socialist outlook in his attitude to the Don. As the Orator in *The Magic Flute* he was superbly impressive; I have heard many finer voices in this supremely difficult part, but no one who interpreted it more convincingly. Old Germont in *La Traviata*, of course, fell to him, and *La Traviata* brings back memories of the Old Vic opera productions in their most ludicrous aspect. *La Traviata* has been an insoluble problem to all operatic producers ever since its first unhappy performance at Venice in 1853; and the more conscientiously the modern producer tackles it, the more difficult it becomes. The Old Vic, I need hardly say, never dreamed of dressing the opera in the costumes of its own day; nor did Covent Garden, except that it was the custom for Melba to wear her latest Paris creations and all her diamonds, while Caruso appeared in what might be called

Vandyck. At the Old Vic everybody wore eighteenth century – 'square-cut' as the wardrobe people would have said. In an operatic wardrobe the whole of the eighteenth century and a good bit of the seventeenth too wore the same fashions – 'square-cut' for the gentlemen, and the ladies in whatever suited them. Wigs were of all sorts; the only thing they had in common was that they never fitted. The scenery consisted of a few general utility sets that had to do for pretty nearly everything; that did not seem to matter very much – it was the furniture that filled me with horror, for every scene seemed to take place in a kitchen. As far as I can remember, it was the worst dressed and mounted opera that I have ever seen in my life. And yet, as we found out later, the wardrobe contained quite a large collection of costumes of various periods, and Mrs. Newman, the wardrobe-mistress, was ready to take the keenest interest in dressing an opera if she was approached as an artist and encouraged to use her ingenuity and imagination. A young *prima donna*, singing the title-part for the first time, said anxiously to Miss Baylis, 'I hope you didn't think I overdid my make-up'. 'Ow now, dear', replied the great lady, 'I always think Violetter ought to look a bit tarty.'

Early in 1914 an appeal had been sent out to ask for £5,000 to carry on the operas at the Vic. It was signed by H.R.H. Princess Christian of Schleswig-Holstein, the most musical of Queen Victoria's daughters, by the Lord Mayor and the Chairman of the L.C.C., followed by a string of musicians whose names make interesting reading at the present day: Thomas Beecham, Arthur Fagge, Edward German, Charles Manners, Fanny Moody (Manners), Nellie Melba, and Henry J. Wood. The modern reader may not perhaps remember Arthur Fagge; he founded and conducted the London Choral Society, the only choral body of its time in London which had the courage to bring out new works. The names of Beecham and Wood stood for pioneering enterprise too, in those days. Moreover, the list is equally interesting for the names which do not appear on it – I leave the reader to think of them and to guess the reasons for their absence. Five thousand pounds would be considered a very modest sum as an endowment for English opera in these days. Miss Baylis did not get more than a few hundreds; the war distracted people's attention to other objects. But she carried everything on all the same, and added Shakespeare to her other burdens; if Shakespeare made a loss, as he very often did, it was the opera which saved the situation. The result was that when the war came to an end opera in English at popular prices was a going concern; not a very grand affair, as I have already suggested, but none the less full of vitality, with an audience that was enthusiastic and steadfast in its attendance.

The general operatic repertory was very properly based on the old standard favourites. Mr. Alfred Dove's tableau performance of *The Rose of Castille* in 1891 must have been about the last time that that ancient opera, first produced in 1857, was ever put on the stage. But up to 1930 at any rate, *The Bohemian Girl*, *Maritana* and *The Lily of Killarney*, together constituting what someone has scoffingly called 'the English *Ring*', were in constant performance. There was a large Irish public in Lambeth (so Miss Baylis said) who always expected *The Lily* in honour of St. Patrick's Day. It was only after Sadler's Wells had got thoroughly well under way that Miss Baylis remarked rather sadly that in view of the new extensions of the

"*Faust & Carmen were sure to fill the house…*"

repertory she did not think she would ever dare to put these three old classics on again.

Faust and *Carmen* were always certain to fill the house, as they are still in every country where opera is performed. It is amusing to read Colonel Mapleson's account of how he produced *Faust* for the first time in England in 1863. This was at Her Majesty's. After the first production in Paris in 1859 one of the Chappells bought the music for reproduction in England for £40 and was told by his partners in London that he had made a very poor purchase. Mr. Frederick Gye, manager of the Italian Opera at Covent Garden, had also been over to Paris to see *Faust* and said there was nothing in it except the 'Soldiers' Chorus'. At Milan it had been a failure; so Mr. Gye would have nothing more to do with it. Mapleson, by a very astute manœuvre, made a success of it; less than a month later Mr. Gye had got it out with his rival company. Mapleson was also the first English manager to see the possibilities of *Carmen*. In 1878 he had heard Minnie Hauk sing *Carmen* at Brussels; he promptly engaged her for Her Majesty's, but here he found himself up against his Italian singers. Costa was willing enough to conduct, but the Italian tenor returned his part saying that he could not think of undertaking a part in which he had no *romanza* and no love-duet except with the *seconda donna*. The baritone said that the part of Escamillo must have been intended for one of the chorus, and that he begged to decline it. The leading soprano said the same about Micaela. Mapleson was an adept at persuasion, and he did induce them all to sing the opera, but the receipts for the first two or three nights were 'most miserable'. For the ingenious dodge by which he secured full houses for both operas the reader must be referred to that fascinating chronicle of operatic absurdities, *The Mapleson Memoirs* (London, 1888).

But Corri was a man of enterprise. In 1914 *Don Giovanni* had been added to the repertory, with scores and parts lent by Charles Manners, whose attitude towards the struggling company at the Vic was always generous and helpful. The Moody-Manners Opera company which he founded in 1898 was in those days one of the most efficient and flourishing of the touring opera companies then on the road. In 1916 Corri staged *Elijah* as an opera; Manners had already done this many years before and the old oratorio was found to be highly effective on the stage. Gounod's *Romeo and Juliet* was another production of the same year. Wagner had already been presented to the Lambeth public in 1912, and *Tannhäuser* was soon followed by *Lohengrin;* both were frequently revived, and in connection with *Tannhäuser* it is interesting to note the first appearance of an Old Vic Ballet, the germ of what has now become for many enthusiastic adorers by far the most exciting activity of Sadler's Wells. For the services of the nymphs and bacchantes whose voluptuous allurements were indispensable to an adequately conducted Venusberg the Annual Report acknowledges its grateful indebtedness to Madame Martha Mayall and her dancers from the Church of the Sacred Heart.

Richard III

*P*UBLICITY, AS theatrical people of to-day understand it, was a thing in which Miss Baylis at first took no interest whatever. When the first Shakespearean seasons were initiated in 1914 her horizon was still bounded by Lambeth; her theatre was run for the population of Lambeth, and she did not care what was said about it outside. She never dreamed of inviting dramatic or musical critics to her first nights; the theatre was always well filled, and why should she waste seats on people who belonged to an entirely different world and would only make fun of her efforts? She had built up her audiences on what one might call a family basis; the best advertisement that she could get was the friendly recommendation of one person to another. From the very first the Victoria Hall had been managed rather on the principles of an early Christian community in the slums of ancient Rome.

Her new actors and actresses, accustomed to the stimulus of press notices, insisted on the systematic organisation of publicity; the opera people – at any rate those who came into the theatre after the end of the war – took the same line, or organised their own publicity through their private friendships in musical journalism. The queer woman who ran a theatre in the Waterloo Road without knowing a thing about Shakespeare suddenly began to find herself something of a celebrity. Before 1914 the Victoria Hall was a 'coffee palace' where the working man and his wife could spend a sober evening listening to *The Bohemian Girl* and watching it represented in the form of tableaux. By 1921 this same place had achieved so widespread a reputation for its productions of Shakespeare that its management was officially invited by the Belgian Government to give a series of performances in Brussels.

It was indeed an astonishing achievement that this institution, which had begun its career solely as an appendage to a religious and social undertaking, should have become not merely a regular theatre, but one of the most important theatres of London, and one that obtained recognition by a foreign Government as the equivalent of a State-supported National Theatre, and this in the comparatively short space of seven years, four of which had been taken up with what was then regarded as the most exhausting war in all our history. Miss Baylis had at the opportune moment provided a theatre and an audience, an audience, too, that was very different in character from the average audience of a West End theatre. It was not really proletarian any longer, but it was still democratic. Nobody appeared in evening dress, and as the difference in price was very little between the stalls and gallery, and the difference in comfort still less, the whole house seemed to acquire a unity of character that was to be observed in the Old Vic and nowhere else. In the West End theatres audiences seldom have any character that gives them a community sense. Most theatres, and especially those which are run for purely commercial purposes with no sense of artistic idealism, depend not on the permanent population of London but on the endless stream of passing visitors, and during a war this instability is greatly accentuated by the presence in London of innumerable members of the fighting forces on a short period of leave which they naturally want to spend in having a good time. Yet even at the present moment, in the sixth year of a war far more devastating, morally and intellectually, as well as physically, than the last one, it is evident that there is still a considerable public which does want to see Shakespeare. To a large extent it wants to see its favourite actors in Shakespeare, but all the same Shakespeare himself is an attraction and the whole attitude of the theatre-going public towards him has changed completely from what it was in the days of Irving and Beerbohm Tree. In those days a certain standard of sumptuousness in mounting was considered indispensable to Shakespearean production; even Granville Barker's settings of *The Winter's Tale*, *Twelfth Night* and *A Midsummer Night's Dream* conformed to that. They were deliberate reactions against older convention, both in decoration and in general outlook, but when we survey what has followed them and what is now accepted as a suitable background for Shakespeare, we cannot help feeling that they belonged to an age that is long past.

For the present day – and not entirely as a wartime measure of economy – simplicity rather than magnificence is what the public expects in a production of Shakespeare, and that is really due to the tradition started during the last war at the Old Vic. Economy was always necessary there, whether in war or in peace. The first Shakespearean productions of 1914 were got up by Matheson Lang and his wife Hutin Britton, with scenery and costumes mostly lent by Matheson Lang himself; they belonged naturally to what I have called the sumptuous school, but Miss Baylis was an adept at borrowing and not returning, and all these were soon merged in her general stock. As soon as the ambition to produce the whole of Shakespeare became manifest, it was obvious that scenery and costume would have to be simplified to the barest necessities, and here the doctrines of William Poel supplied helpful direction, though they were not carried out with his own pedantic accuracy.

Who first suggested that the Vic ought to produce the whole of Shakespeare I do not know; probably it was not so much one man's idea as a growing consciousness in the minds of everyone working in the theatre, Miss Baylis herself included. Shakespeare, like Mr. Shaw, might have classed his own plays as 'pleasant' and 'unpleasant'; anyone who sets out to put the whole of Shakespeare on the stage has to face the 'unpleasant' plays and do what he can to make them acceptable. And the production of these is only possible with simplified scenery. For one thing, no manager of the old days could ever have contemplated staging *Timon of Athens* or *Pericles* with photographically realistic scenery in the hopes of a long run; but when all scenery and costume were so simple that both could be used again and again for all sorts of different plays a few performances of the unfamiliar works could be risked. Even if there was a loss on these, the deficit would be paid by *Faust* and *Maritana*.

In October, 1914, Mr. and Mrs. Matheson Lang produced *The Taming of the Shrew*, *Hamlet* and *The Merchant of Venice*, followed in November by Ben Greet's production of *The Tempest;* later in November Estelle Stead and Andrew Leigh produced *The Merry Wives of Windsor*. A series of Ben Greet productions came next – *The Comedy of Errors*, *Twelfth Night*, *A Midsummer Night's Dream* (for Christmas) and *Macbeth*, all between November, 1914, and January, 1915. *As You Like It* (February, 1915) was staged by Estelle Stead and Andrew Leigh; *The Winter's Tale* and *Othello* by Ben Greet in March. The last play of that season was *Julius Cæsar*, produced in April by J. Fisher White. From the autumn of 1915 to the spring of 1918 all productions were directed by Ben Greet, and in the long list which follows we note more and more of the less familiar plays: *Romeo and Juliet*, *King Henry V*, *King Richard III;* (1916) *Much Ado About Nothing*, *King Henry VIII*, *King Richard II*, *Two Gentlemen of Verona;* (1917) *King John*, *King Henry IV* (Part II); (1918) *King Lear* and *Cymbeline*. For the winter of 1918-19 the producer was G. R. Foss – 'he knew as much about acting Shakespeare as Irving, and as much about the human heart as Browning' (W. Bridges Adams); his productions were *Measure for Measure*, *Love's Labour's Lost*, and the First Part of *King Henry IV*. There was only one new Shakespeare production in 1920 – *Coriolanus* (Russell Thorndike and Charles Warburton). Robert Atkins took over the productions from May, 1921, to November, 1923: *Pericles*, *All's Well that Ends Well;* (1922) *Timon of Athens*, *Antony and Cleopatra;* (1923) all three parts of *King Henry VI* in two performances, *Titus Andronicus*, *Troilus and Cressida*. It should be noted that from 1916 onwards there were frequent performances of *Hamlet* 'in its entirety', always given in the afternoons on account of the enormous length of the play.

As soon as the war was at an end there was naturally a general revival of activity throughout the theatrical world, and the Old Vic had no monopoly of Shakespeare; but the public and even the critics began gradually to acknowledge that the Vic productions had a character of their own, a character well indicated by the critic of *Truth* as 'simpleness and duty'. Miss Viola Tree staged a curious revival of *The Tempest* at His Majesty's; some of the scenery was new and modernistic, but about half of it obviously out of the stock which she had inherited. There was a great deal of incidental music, and Miss Tree herself appeared as a singer in the masque; but as the music ranged from Purcell and Arne to Sullivan and Arthur Bliss it could hardly be said to have much unity of style. Sullivan's music for *The Tempest* is one of the best pieces of craftsmanship that he ever produced; but I could only wish that Bliss had been given a free hand to compose music for the entire play, for his opening scene (the shipwreck) was marvellously dramatic and original. As to the acting, I recall only the exquisite beauty of Henry Ainley's swift and rhythmical declamation of the speeches of Prospero, to which the leisurely and tedious facetiousness of the comedians made a dismal contrast, and the singular graciousness and charm of Miss Tree in a comparatively unimportant part.

At the moment of the poet's birthday in 1921 there was not only the Shakespeare season at the Old Vic, but the Birthday Festival at Stratford with seven plays directed by Bridges Adams, and a highly coloured repertory of Shakespeare under Mr. Fagan at the Court Theatre. The example of the Vic was encouraging even to West End managers, but the spirit of poetry was only to be found in Lambeth and at Stratford. At the Old Vic *The Tempest* was played throughout in one and the same unchanging scene, a background of rocks and a pale sky, seen under various lightings; this not only saved time but concentrated all attention on the play itself, and the company was much commended for the clearness with which all the words were spoken.

As far back as the days of Miss Cons it was observable that all sorts of people outside the theatre were becoming aware of the Vic as an institution which might be exploited for their own ends, religious, social or even artistic. As soon as Shakespeare had established a firm footing there it became clear that the Old Vic was no longer a convenient site to be captured and utilised; it was a permanent home of serious drama, and in a position to offer hospitality to new movements and ideas which otherwise would have had little or no chance of finding show room in London. And since the Vic had begun its reformed career under definitely religious auspices and was still managed by an unashamedly religious woman, it was only natural that the religious play should find a very cordial welcome there. The nineteenth century had been decidedly prudish with regard to religious plays; its religious teaching was largely obsessed by the doctrine of 'reverence', and reverence was always associated with particular words, rather than with the ideas that lay behind them. To attempt to explain the psychology of this attitude, to trace its history and its effect on literature and drama would be an interesting study, but one that is certainly far beyond the scope of this book. We can only draw attention to the long-standing prejudice of devout people against the theatre itself as a temple of wickedness, a prejudice certainly due more to the behaviour of audiences than to what was said and represented on the stage. In the eighteenth century and for a good part of the nineteenth clerical authority was able to suppress theatrical performances during Lent, or on certain days thereof, as well as during Holy Week. It was for this reason that Handel started performing oratorios in his theatre on nights when operas were forbidden; but it is curious to note that *Israel in Egypt* and *Messiah*, the only oratorios of his in which the words are taken direct from the Bible, caused great offence among the devout of those days, because they considered it blasphemous to sing the actual words of sacred Scripture in a building normally associated with Italian opera. They had no objection to the other oratorios, in which Biblical stories are treated more or less on operatic lines and the characters made to sing operatic airs in a very elegantly operatic English. None the less, the eighteenth century had its religious drama; in 1793 Tate Wilkinson produced at Hull, Doncaster and Leeds two biblical plays by Hannah More, the friend of Garrick and Dr. Johnson, *Moses in the Bulrushes* and *Daniel in the Lions' Den*. The Wesleyans and Methodists, he tells us, gave their cordial approval to them, but he was 'barked at' by all the preachers of the Established Church. Wilkinson demurely announced the plays as 'connected with the opera of *Rosina*, which, it is allowed, by no means degrades what it accompanies, since the Book of Ruth furnished the subject'. And it is clear that Tate Wilkinson took the theatre quite as seriously as Lilian Baylis did; he stoutly defends its morality, and observes that although the Apostles reproved all vices – 'nothing escaped them – but we hear not of any poet or actor who received any reprimand from them'.

William Poel converted the religious world by his discovery and revival of *Everyman*. From the first he surrounded it with the right atmosphere, dressing the players in more or less Elizabethan costumes, performing the play in picturesque halls with incidental music drawn from Elizabethan composers and arranged by Arnold Dolmetsch. He was even considered to have 'spiritualised' the play and to have removed it still further from theatrical realism by assigning the part of Everyman himself to a lady. *Everyman* soon generated its imitators, as well as encouraging the revival of other genuine mysteries and moralities of the Middle Ages. In December, 1913, Miss Baylis was anxious to welcome *Eager Heart*, a very sentimental modern Nativity play by a Miss Buckton which achieved great popularity in devout circles for a time, as it was not too difficult for amateurs. In recent years religious plays of all kinds, both mediæval and modern, have frequently been acted in churches, a proceeding which in Victorian days would have been considered so blasphemous that the very idea of it would have been positively unmentionable.

From religious plays the transition is natural to Greek plays. Professor Gilbert Murray's translations had begun to make Euripides fashionable, and in November, 1919, the theatre was crowded for a series of afternoon performances of *The Trojan Women*. The main attraction was, of course, Sybil Thorndike, whose interpretation of the part of Hecuba made a powerful appeal to a war-weary audience. Whether it will ever be possible to solve the problem of the chorus in English revivals of Greek tragedy is doubtful. The critic of *The Athenæum*, during the immediate post-war years the organ of the young intellectuals under the leadership of John Middleton Murry, was amusingly scornful of the Vic's 'chorus of six ladies, grouped in careful Royal Academy poses, moving in well-rehearsed Dalcroze rhythms, beating their breasts with correct Delsarte expressiveness', and he particularly deplored the semi-musical 'chanting', as if the actresses were trying to intone 'a droning tune designed by some inept amateur with a taste for folksongs'.

It was inevitable that sooner or later a reaction against eternal Shakespeare should set in, all the more since the unfamiliar plays had generally resulted in financial losses. Outside the Vic a new society had been founded by the Reverend Montague Summers for the private performance of Elizabethan and Restoration plays. The Phœnix, as it was called, brought back to the professional theatre a good many plays which had already been staged several years before by the undergraduate actors of the Marlowe Society at Cambridge, founded in 1909. But the Cambridge performances had been a good deal hampered by the censorship of an all too well-read Vice-Chancellor; The Phœnix, acting on Sunday afternoons to a congregation of private subscribers, could present its plays unexpurgated, and this naturally gave a great impetus to the revival of interest in Restoration comedy, an interest which has been pretty steadily maintained during the last twenty years. But it was some time before Miss Baylis could bring herself to allow Congreve on the hallowed boards of the Old Vic.

The most striking of the new experiments that were tried was Ibsen's *Peer Gynt*, a drama which, like Goethe's *Egmont*, was known to English audiences only by name, through its association with the incidental music in both cases frequently to be heard at popular concerts. The production of *Peer Gynt* under Robert Atkins, with Russell Thorndike in the title part, was the first complete performance of the work in this country, and Grieg's music was made an integral part of it. Corri had arranged it with his usual skill and ingenuity. As a concert suite the familiar pieces had rather outlived their popularity; most musical people would have said that they had heard them too often and never wished to hear them again. To hear them in the theatre, each in its proper place, was a new and delightful experience; the music intensified all the dramatic effects, especially in those scenes where the poet leads us unexpectedly into an atmosphere of the fantastic and unreal, and the words and actions of the stage, admirably fitted in to it by a company of actors of unusual rhythmical sensibility, gave a new depth and poignancy to the music.

A few years later an even more daring experiment was tried with a new English version of Goethe's *Faust*, translated and adapted by Graham and Tristan Rawson.

This too must have been the first time that anyone had ever attempted to put the whole of Goethe's drama on the stage in English; to compress the two parts in their entirety into one evening's representation would have been utterly impossible, but this version seized on the essentials and gave a remarkably successful idea of the remote and 'undramatic' second part as well as of the more familiar first. From a literary point of view the translation was surprisingly good; students of Goethe have

Peer Gynt 1944

generally held that his language is absolutely untranslatable, but the brothers Rawson achieved a version which was always in good English, effective when spoken on the stage, and in its rhythms and cadences unmistakably caught the characteristic style and personality of the poet.

The outside activities of the Vic Shakespeare company during these years deserve consideration, for every time that the company appeared elsewhere it was an affirmation of the Vic's existence and standing in the world of drama. In 1916 the Vic furnished a Shakespeare company for the Festival at Stratford-on-Avon. In 1921

1 *Royal Cobourg Theatre, 1818 (renamed Royal Victoria Hall, 1833).* 2 *Royal Victoria Hall. Visit of Their Royal Highnesses the Prince and Princess of Wales, March 3rd, 1910.* 3 *Laying the Stage Cloth at Old Vic.* 4 *Old Vic—Lithograph by Wilfrid Walter.* 5 *Old Vic Safety Curtain, by Robert Medley.*

1 *Ben Greet, Producer, Old Vic, 1916-18.* **2** *Sybil Thorndike.* **3** *Charles Corri, Conductor.* **4** *Russell Thorndike, Producer, Old Vic, 1919.* **5** *Andrew Leigh, Producer, Old Vic, 1925-29.* **6** *Robert Atkins, Producer, Old Vic, 1919-25.* [Photo: Sasha.] **7** *Harcourt Williams, Producer, Old Vic, 1929-33.* [Photo: Claude Harris.] **8** *Henry Cass, Producer, Old Vic, 1934-35.* [Photo: Kenelm Harvey Ltd.] **9** *Ninette de Valois, Director of Ballet, Sadler's Wells.* [Photo: Anthony.] **10** *Joan Cross, Director of Opera.* [Photo: John Vickers.] **11** *Tyrone Guthrie, Producer, Old Vic, 1933-34, 1936-45.* [Photo: Howard Coster.]

the Belgian Minister of Fine Arts formally invited the Vic company to go over to Brussels in June and give a series of Shakespeare performances under royal patronage at the Théâtre du Parc; this was practically equivalent to a recognition of the Vic as the British National Theatre. In 1923 the minute-book records that suggestions were being made for a visit of the company to Copenhagen, but this had to be laid aside, as the necessary financial guarantees were not forthcoming. In the summer of 1924 Mr. C. B. Cochran engaged the Vic players for a month's Shakespeare at the New Oxford Theatre (in London) in connection with the British Empire Exhibition. It is amusing to compare the Old Vic's official annual report with Mr. Cochran's own reminiscences – not that there is any divergence between them on matters of positive fact. The report informs us that the audiences were very small, but gradually increased in numbers; they were always enthusiastic, and no doubt if the season had continued for long enough (at Mr. Cochran's expense) the house would eventually have been full. Mr. Cochran knew perfectly well what he was doing, and accepted the risk, but one month was enough. There was, as he observes, no prominent star, or any real novelty; 'it was Shakespeare or nothing, and Shakespeare lost, much to my disappointment'. In a letter which he sent later to the Press, Mr. Cochran opined that 'it is perfectly obvious that the name of Shakespeare terrifies the British play-going public'. The public was not grateful, but the management of the Vic certainly was, for a characteristic act of courage on the part of a great impresario.

If London at that time failed to appreciate Shakespeare, the provincial centres were always ready to welcome him. Every year tours were arranged in the summer to Manchester, Blackpool, Newcastle and other towns, generally in the north of England where it has long been evident that music and drama are far more intelligently appreciated than in the south. At the time these northern tours were regarded mainly as a convenient way of keeping the company together and giving them some sort of a living. Miss Baylis, of course, took no financial risks and always insisted on a local guarantee. The opera company did a certain amount of touring too, but not as much as the drama company. The real importance of these tours did not become apparent until the period of the present war when the entire organisation of the Vic and Wells in London was disrupted and the only chance of survival lay in continuous touring. The story of these years belongs to a later chapter.

The Vic had built up its prosperity and its reputation on the principle of being 'the home of Shakespeare', but after the whole series of Shakespeare plays had once been produced, an inevitable reaction set in, and successive directors of drama tended more and more towards modern plays. Harcourt Williams became director in 1929 and brought a good many new ideas and methods to bear on Shakespearean production. They were severely criticised, but they justified themselves by attracting greatly

F

increased audiences. Like Granville Barker in the years before the war, he insisted on a much more rapid style of declamation; another innovation was his use of different levels on the stage and the construction of a staircase from the orchestra pit to serve as an additional approach to it. The two marble staircases at the sides of the orchestra at Sadler's Wells were probably suggested by these new requirements. Under this regime Bernard Shaw made his first approved entry into the Old Vic with two of his smaller plays – *The Dark Lady of the Sonnets* and *Androcles and the Lion*. Among the Shakespeare productions may be noted *A Midsummer Night's Dream* acted in Elizabethan costumes with that curious jumble of folksongs and other oddments which Cecil Sharp strung together for Granville Barker's famous production. The Old Vic public seems, however, to have preferred Mendelssohn, to whom a return was wisely made in later revivals of the play.

In 1931 Sadler's Wells Theatre was opened, and for the first two years drama and opera were given there alternately, but it soon became evident that it would be much more satisfactory to confine drama to the Old Vic and give opera and ballet only at Sadler's Wells. The dramatic company must have been as heartily relieved to get rid of their partner as the opera company were. The two departments were at this time practically strangers to one another, and each of them found the other perpetually in the way as long as they were obliged to do all their work in the same building, all the more so as neither of the two theatres, despite all the money that had been poured out on them, was structurally adequate for the activities of even one company.

A new director of drama appeared on the scene in 1933 – Tyrone Guthrie, described in the Report as 'the youngest producer the Vic has ever had'. Modern plays now began to occupy an ever-increasing space in the repertory, and it was found that Shakespeare needed stars of a certain magnitude to keep him going. The home of Shakespeare had almost become the home of Shaw. Needless to say the play of his which appealed most powerfully to Miss Baylis was *Saint Joan*. Along with Shaw came Oscar Wilde; there was a long run of *The Importance of Being Earnest*. Ibsen was almost as firmly established as Shaw, and in 1933 the Vic for the first time presented its audience with a play of Tchekov – *The Cherry Orchard*. Some of the older dramatists were suggested and discussed, but not always accepted for performance. Marlowe's *Edward II* was considered 'unsuitable'. *Volpone* might have met with the same fate, but fortunately for the Governors a production of it at another theatre gave them a good excuse for not performing it. Congreve, however, was allowed to pass, surprising as it may seem. Miss Baylis had many qualms of conscience about allowing *Love for Love* to be performed in her theatre; it had been revived by the Phœnix Society and it had also been performed at the Festival Theatre in

Cambridge during the tenancy of that most audacious of managers, Mr. Terence Gray. Kneeling at her roll-top desk she sought guidance, and the still small voice told her that Congreve would certainly be very good business for the theatre. Conscience relieved, she authorised the production, and it followed as a natural consequence that Congreve's reputation was whitewashed once for all: he was acted at

young soldiers carry ammunition...
The old ones carry chocolate
(Arms & the Man : 44)

the Old Vic, and the Lambeth judgment signified authoritatively that he was as innocent as Goldsmith or Sheridan.

In June, 1937, the British Council, a body which had recently come into being under the ægis of the Foreign Office for the encouragement of representative British culture in foreign countries, arranged a visit of the Vic Shakespeare company to Elsinore in Denmark, in order that *Hamlet* might be acted for a week on the battlements of the historic castle. This was directed by Tyrone Guthrie. The performances being in the open air were at the mercy of the weather, which was for the most part stormy, but the company struggled bravely against the elements and were enthralled at the opportunity of acting in such romantic surroundings. This *Hamlet* was performed in Shakespearean costumes, but Guthrie had other ideas for the presentation of *Hamlet* which were to be realised a little later. In May, 1938, the British Council and the Egyptian Government invited the Vic to undertake a season of three weeks in Cairo, with the possibility of extending the tour to Alexandria, Malta, Rome and Florence. Guthrie at once suggested that one of the plays to be acted there should be *Hamlet* in modern dress. *Hamlet* in modern dress was, of course, no very new idea; Barry Jackson had already carried it out with great success at the Birmingham Repertory Theatre and Leopold Jessner had at once treated *Hamlet* in the same way at Berlin, although the German conception of modern dress Shakespeare was very different from the English one, as the manners and customs adopted were those of the court of Emperor William II. Some of the Vic Governors were simply horrified at this project, and it was suggested that to act *Hamlet* in modern dress at Rome or Florence would probably be disastrous. It was the fact that *The Apple-Cart*, when acted in Italian at Milan, had provoked definite hostility; English audiences may be able to take a jesting view of politics, but in a country where all political situations are chronically precarious, the monarchy included, and where political corruption has always been regarded as the normal and natural principle of government, official circles (and their attendant journalists) do not like to see ministers made ridiculous on the stage. The same attitude towards political blasphemy had been exhibited in 1934 when Malipiero's opera *Il Figliuol Cambiato* had been removed from the stage after one performance by order of the authorities, because it was a modern fairy-tale in which not only a king but his prime minister in cutaway coat and striped trousers had been turned into figures of fun. Worse than that, it was even suggested that to play *Hamlet* in modern dress would be an infringement of the traditions of the Old Vic – traditions which after all could not possibly date further back than 1914! To the credit of the Governors it may be recorded that they eventually agreed to Guthrie's proposal and to take their chances with a fascist audience. *Hamlet* was put into rehearsal and was the outstanding feature of the autumn season; moreover, it was given in its entirety, and proved so popular that its run had to be considerably extended.

The Mediterranean tour started in January, 1939; as the journeys were effected mostly by sea, performances began in Lisbon, where the reception of the company was more than cordial. In the previous month a certain agitation had been got up in London by ardent anti-fascists who threatened to boycott the Old Vic altogether if the company went to perform in fascist Italy. The Governors refused to be drawn into a political controversy and astutely pushed the entire responsibility on to the shoulders of the British Council. From Lisbon the company proceeded to Milan, where *Hamlet* was so successful at the Teatro Manzoni that it had to be repeated each night, the other plays being taken off. Guthrie was invited by the management to go out to Milan later on and produce *Cæsar and Cleopatra* for an Italian company.

At Rome and Naples they had almost equal success, and after Italy they visited Cairo, Alexandria, Athens and Malta. Among the other plays acted were *Henry V*, *The Rivals*, *Man and Superman*, and *Trelawny of the Wells*.

Miss Baylis died, rather suddenly, on November 25, 1937. The work of the theatre went on just the same; it was what she herself would have desired. People who had no inside knowledge of her work said that neither of her two theatres could possibly survive her. If that had been in the least degree true, it would have written her off as one whose life-work had been a failure. The two theatres did survive, and even at the present moment, in the sixth year of a war, with both buildings closed, the theatres, as organisations, survive still and are flourishing more than ever. They are the living monuments to her memory. Her own work, as a matter of fact, was ended, just as that of Miss Cons had ended before her. There was no sudden change of policy or break with the past for the moment, and when the break came, it was forced upon the two theatres by the stress of war. If Miss Baylis had lived longer, she might very likely have exercised a restraining hand on the ambitions of producers and conductors at both theatres. In all three departments—for by this time the Sadler's Wells Ballet had come into existence and had indeed leapt into fame with astonishing *élévation* – the consciousness was becoming felt that the 'Vic-Wells', as the double organisation now came to be commonly called, had ceased to be a 'people's theatre' and was doing its best to fulfil the functions of a state-subsidised national theatre and opera house catering for highly educated audiences. Everyone connected with the two theatres was working their hardest to raise the level of performances to the highest possible pitch. Prices were gradually raised, although those of the gallery remained as low as was economically possible; if 'the people' still felt inclined to come, they were heartily welcome. As long as Miss Baylis lived, it was tacitly assumed that the founder's aims were still being pursued without divergence; after she died, questions of fundamental policy began to be discussed, though at first only in a very tentative and non-committal way. Indeed, even now, when a decision on fundamental policy would seem to be a matter of positive urgency, the general tendency is to 'wait and see', and to postpone all decisions, and as far as possible, all formal discussion, until the war is definitely over and conditions of life have 'returned to normal'—if they ever do so.

The practical results of all these ambitions, as might have been expected, was financial loss at both theatres and a considerable accumulation of debt. The situation was made worse by the general political unrest. The threat of war was perpetually in the air, and every theatre in London was affected by it. At the end of the season of 1938-39 both theatres showed losses of considerably over £6,000.

As SOON as the war of 1914-1918 was over Miss Baylis began to make plans for an enlargement of the operatic repertory, and since *Don Giovanni* had been something of a popular success in 1914 it occurred to her that the time had come to revive *The Marriage of Figaro*, all the more since a new light soprano had just joined the company, Muriel Gough, who before the war had had six years' experience of work in German opera houses. Miss Baylis suggested that Miss Gough should herself produce *Figaro* as well as undertake the part of Susanna. Miss Gough modestly declined; she would be delighted to sing Susanna, but she thought she knew of a much more suitable producer in the person of Clive Carey, who was a man of varied accomplishments – he had had practical experience both as an opera singer and as an actor in plays, and was a notable composer as well. He had produced *The Magic Flute* for the Cambridge performance of 1911 and had himself sung the part of Papageno. On being approached by Miss Baylis he agreed to produce *Figaro* for her and sing the part of Figaro too, provided that she would make use of a new translation that I had made in the summer of 1915 at the suggestion of T. C. Fairbairn, who before the war ran an opera school in St. John's Wood in partnership with Hermann Grünbaum. Miss Baylis hesitated about accepting a new translation. I do not think she ever read it, and I doubt whether Corri ever did either; her immediate reaction to the suggestion was that it would be a great labour and expense to copy the new words into the old books, and that it would be most unfair to a voluntary chorus to ask them to learn new words, all the more since nobody ever heard the words that the chorus sang in any opera. The principal singers, too, would certainly very much resent having to learn a new version and, indeed, would probably say that to learn a new set of words was absolutely impossible in practice. That difficulty was solved by getting together a cast of singers none of whom – except possibly Ewart Beech and Sam Harrison – had ever sung in the opera before. It was a great advantage, too, in another way; the singers came to rehearsal with no preconceived notions or dim recollections of established traditions, so that the opera could be studied afresh as if it had been an entirely new and unknown work. The one point on which Corri and Miss Baylis stood firm was that the opera must not exceed the normal time-limit, which was something under three hours. *Figaro*, if performed 'in its entirety', would probably take well over four hours; it is an exceptionally long opera for its period. The recitatives had already been reduced to the barest minimum of spoken dialogue; in addition to the cuts that are usual in nearly all opera houses Corri demanded the sacrifice of the sextet in Act III – perhaps the greatest masterpiece of comic ensemble ever composed by Mozart or by anyone else – and a large slice out of the last finale, both of these musical items having to be replaced by the shortest possible explanatory dialogue.

The general principle of the Vic was that operatic rehearsals should be avoided as far as possible, mainly on account of the ever-increasing expense of the orchestra, but also out of consideration for the Shakespeare company who had an equal claim to the stage. Moreover, Miss Baylis was accustomed to pay her singers the lowest possible fees and this could only be excused on the ground that she always allowed them every possible opportunity of earning money by outside concert engagements. She was quite unprepared for the amount of rehearsal that Carey demanded as a matter of course. Luckily the singers were all very keen as soon as they realised his aims and intentions; a good many extra rehearsals took place in a disused public-house in Oakley Street which Miss Baylis had secured as a store-room and extra practice-room, and still more were held at Carey's own flat, until all the ensemble movements, both in music and in action, went with a precision and vivacity hitherto quite unknown at the Vic. Another thing on which Carey insisted was the clear enunciation of all the words, and the company were rewarded unexpectedly for that by bursts of laughter from the audience even in the middle of an ensemble. Superior members of the audience were gravely shocked at this; on the rare occasions when *Figaro* had been performed in Italian at Covent Garden it would never have occurred to anyone to laugh. As to scenery and costumes we had to be content with what there was in stock, and for a straightforward work like *Figaro* the Vic wardrobe was quite adequately supplied; all that was needed was a sense of judgment in choosing out of what was available. The stock scenery did well enough too; in any case we were determined to avoid the Dresden China prettiness with which Mozart was almost always staged in the German court theatres. Mahler had set a good example at Vienna; most German conductors and producers spoke of it with horror, even twenty years later, calling it 'the "red" *Figaro*' as if it had been a communist demonstration (in the Imperial opera house!). We were quite unable to reproduce its magnificence, but we were determined to capture something of the squalor of its first scene – the servants' bedroom, so cramped and uncomfortable that Figaro might well go down on hands and knees to measure up if there would be room for a double bed in it.

The success of *Figaro* was encouraging, and Miss Baylis saw at once that she had captured an opera producer of genius. He now proposed to put on *The Magic Flute*, an opera which before the Cambridge performance of 1911 had become almost legendary in this country. Most people could think of it only as an Italian opera notorious for inconsequence of plot and absurdity of language as well as for two solo parts, high soprano and low bass respectively, which made such exceptional demands on the compass of the singers that voices adequate for them could only be discovered perhaps once in a hundred years. The Cambridge performance at any rate showed that there were plenty of singers who could tackle these parts and it also showed that the opera was not so nonsensical as had been imagined; besides that it presented the work with drastically simplified scenery which saved much waste of time between the numerous scenes and also gave considerable dignity to the whole stage picture. If Cambridge could perform *The Magic Flute*, obviously the Old Vic could do as well if not better. Orchestral parts and most of the dresses were borrowed from Cambridge; Steuart Wilson, who had sung Tamino at Cambridge, was imported for the occasion, and the scenery was arranged as simply and formally as possible. Once more Mozart proved a decisive popular success, and from that moment *Figaro* and *The Magic Flute* became indispensable features of every season's repertory; up to 1939 one or the other, if not both, was given every year.

Just before our production of *The Magic Flute* a remarkable performance of the same opera had been given by the boys of an elementary school in Glengall Road, Isle of Dogs, under the direction of a very enterprising schoolmaster and pioneer in educational matters, Mr. C. T. Smith. Already before the previous war he had had the idea of a school opera, and had given a performance of *Faust* with a mixed company of boys and girls. He published a book about his operatic efforts, which came into my hands; the next thing was that my own book on Mozart's operas came into his, and within a week of reading it he had made up his mind to perform *The Magic Flute*, the ethical and indeed 'educational' aspect of which made it singularly suitable in his opinion for a school performance. He made his own arrangement of the opera for boys' voices, shortening here and there and cutting out the *coloratura* passages of the Queen of Night. All the boys learned all the parts, so that under-studies were at once available, and indeed at the actual performances the Queen and Monostatos exchanged parts between the two acts. I remember that on one afternoon the Queen had to leave the rehearsal early to go and sell evening papers in the streets. The chorus was made up of all the minor characters, who came on in whatever costume they happened to be wearing, ladies, genii (there were six of each instead of three), priests, slaves, or men in armour. Costumes and scenery were all home-made, of course, mostly by the mothers of the performers; but Mr. Smith took his opera company to the British Museum to make sure that the Egyptian architecture and dresses were correct. Papageno had made his own costume by the simple expedient of cutting a hole in the middle of a blanket and adorning himself with the feathers of a domestic fowl; he looked rather like a Red Indian Chief, and needless to say was the delight of the audience as he played the part with the assurance of a born comedian. The curious thing is that in school (so Mr. Smith told me) he was a rather difficult boy, inclined to be morose and sulky; singing the part of Papageno released his inhibitions and he was able to realise his inward self. Among other distinguished spectators who found their none too easy way to the Isle of Dogs was our own *prima donna*, who said to me afterwards, 'I've sung in this opera I don't know how many times, but this is the first time that I've really understood it'. When we performed *The Magic Flute* at the Vic we invited all the boys from the Glengall

— *a wild-looking girl*

Road school to a matinée and tea; Miss Gough said we ought to have taken all our own company to the Isle of Dogs to learn how to interpret Mozart.

One of the delightful things about opera at the Vic was the positively affectionate attitude of the audience towards its favourite singers. Even in pouring rain there would always be a group of young people from the gallery waiting outside the stage door to say good-night to Miss Gough or Miss Kennard (Pamina) and present them with a handful of chrysanthemums. They were very ready to talk, too, and one evening in the winter a wild-looking girl rushed up to Clive Carey as he came out and scolded him soundly for running about the stage barefooted. 'You'll catch your death of cold. Haven't you got any slippers?' 'I had some once, but they got worn out and I never saw any others that I liked.' 'I shall knit you a pair; what colour would you like?' Green was the colour agreed on, and after about a fortnight a pair of green knitted slippers was left at the stage door. We never saw the girl again; nobody knew her name, and there was no way of thanking her except to wear the slippers on the stage at the next performance. I could only think of Kundry in the first act of *Parsifal*.

We found that these people from the gallery were astonishingly well-informed about opera in general; how they acquired their knowledge I cannot imagine, for the operas that they asked for were not in the current repertory of Covent Garden, nor even in that of the Carl Rosa Company. 'Can't you give us *Norma*? and *Così fan tutte* or *Don Giovanni*? *Norma*, we felt, was rather beyond us, and *Così fan tutte* as well; but it was simply an obvious duty to these gallery folk to give them *Don Giovanni*. That summer Clive Carey went out to Royat in France to help Jean de Reszke with his singing classes, and I went with him, to make a new translation of *Don Giovanni*. Clive sang the words through as I wrote them, to make sure that they were singable, and in the evenings we used to go round to the Hotel Majestic and talk about the opera with the *maestro*, who would reel off whole scenes of it from memory, without accompaniment, just as a *sotto voce* illustration to his most illuminating discourse.

The production of *Don Giovanni* at the Vic presented various points of novelty. In the first place we made up our minds quite definitely that it was to be presented as a comic opera and not as a romantic tragedy. A distinguished German critic was present, and some of his remarks are interesting as showing how far removed the Vic production was from orthodox German tradition. It is true that orthodox German tradition had been pretty completely upset as far

Cherubino in
"Marriage of Figaro"

back as 1896, when the opera was given in the Residenz-Theater at Munich, where the revolving stage had just been installed for the first time especially to cope with the scenic difficulties of this particular opera. The outstanding feature of the Munich performances was the restoration of the original finale at the end of Act II, a scene always omitted in conventional performances.* One thing that surprised and delighted the German critic was that the characters were always given the opportunity of sitting down whenever that might be appropriate, as, for instance, when Donna Anna relates the story of her nocturnal misadventure to Don Ottavio, and also in the ballroom scene. In Germany, he said, the whole opera is given without a single opportunity to sit down. He saw *The Magic Flute* and *Figaro* too; what impressed him in the former was first of all the concentration on the significance of the story and the way in which it was made clear – clearer perhaps than in the German – by the new English translation, and he was charmed, too, with the lightness and eighteenth century grace that was given to *Figaro* by the suppleness of the English language, which in its rhythms at any rate, if indeed not in its vowel sounds, comes much nearer to the original Italian than German can ever do. Other German critics, especially after 1933, attended opera performances either at the Old Vic or at Sadler's Wells, and they invariably said that what pleased them most was the complete freedom in all our productions from the stock traditions of business on the German stage; in every case they 'felt as if they were seeing a new opera'.

We certainly did our best to make *Don Giovanni* a new opera, not merely by restoring the comic finale, but by dressing the opera as near as we could in the style of Goya. Miss Baylis, of course, would allow no expenditure of money; practically everything had to be done out of stock. But our good friend J. B. Trend, now Professor of Spanish at Cambridge, sent us picture postcards of Goya pictures in Madrid, as well as a few genuine Spanish combs and mantillas; he even instructed the ladies how to wear them. The ingenious Mrs. Newman made one new dress only, copied all by herself from a picture postcard – the white dress with a scarlet bolero worn by Miss Gough as Zerlina, with a series of flounces of Nottingham lace. The late eighteenth century costumes gave quite a new aspect to the opera, all the more as the Commendatore did not appear in the conventional full armour, but in eighteenth century clothes.

* Stanford, of course, restored it when he performed *Don Giovanni* at the Royal College of Music.

'He ought to look like Handel,' I said, 'both with and without his wig.' Miss Baylis was quite unable to mount him on a horse; the cemetery could be indicated only by a couple of very conventional cypresses and a stone column or two. The Commendatore stood motionless – later on he was allowed to sit, as standing was too exhausting – on a pedestal, dressed in eighteenth century style, but all white like marble, with a toga borrowed from Julius Cæsar thrown over his shoulders. When he walked in to the supper scene, someone said to me that he looked like a statesman out of Westminster Abbey. There was no question about his dignity; it was overwhelming. As the infernal regions were still sublet to Morley College, it was impossible for any traps to be used, or for fire to come up from below as at Munich; so Don Giovanni was escorted to Hell by a group of sinister black figures vaguely suggesting the Inquisition, led by our admirably grotesque interpreter of Don Basilio and Monostatos, Ewart Beech, an expert, one might say, in stage clericalism.

It was very seldom, in old days, that any contacts were made between the opera people and the Shakespeare company, but on this occasion the opera was enormously indebted to the kind help given by Robert Atkins, who was keenly interested in the production of *Don Giovanni* and always ready to make useful suggestions about scenery and lighting. He saw at once that the opera needed something more than an old-fashioned conventional presentation, and was wonderfully ingenious at obtaining quite new effects by the rearrangement of old oddments of scenery and the clever disposition of curtains. He very cordially appreciated, too, our firm determination never to let the stage be kept waiting during a change of scene, either in *Don Giovanni* or in *The Magic Flute*. These performances thereby brought about a certain re-education of our audiences. In old days every separate number would have been applauded and the opera interrupted while the singer came forward to bow her acknowledgments, as in provincial Italian theatres, but from now onwards operas were carefully produced in a way that prevented the audience from applauding; song merged almost imperceptibly into dialogue and the audience began to take a new pleasure in the swift continuity of the action.

It was said in the old days that the state of enmity between Montagues and Capulets was nothing as compared to the hatred and jealousy prevailing between the Cobourg Theatre and the Surrey, but in the winter of 1919-20 the Surrey returned once more to life as an English opera house under the management of Messrs. Fairbairn and Miln, and contrived at the same time to be always on the friendliest of terms with the Old Vic. This new management had the courage to bring out an entirely new opera by a British composer, Nicholas Gatty's setting of *The Tempest*. The staging of it presented very difficult problems, and at one moment led to a most embarrassing situation. Alonzo and his party had to come on in a ship and sing a good deal of music from the deck of it. *The Flying Dutchman* was also in the Miln-Fairbairn company's repertory, and a couple of practicable ships on wheels had been acquired from the Carl Rosa. One of these was used for Gatty's opera, but the stage-manager had not allowed for the heavy rake of the old Surrey stage, and no sooner

— continued to sing as if nothing had happened

had the ship entered from the prompt wing than it proceeded to roll swiftly down towards the footlights, doing considerable damage to the canvas sea in which its wheels were entangled. However, a few brave mariners leapt boldly into the foaming waters and pushed the ship uphill again towards safer regions, while those on board continued to sing as if nothing was happening. *The Tempest* was taken on by the Old Vic two years later, as a suitable opera with which to celebrate Shakespeare's birthday, for Miss Baylis, accustomed as she was to the observance of Saints' days in church, always liked to have something of a calendar of anniversaries in the theatre. Under Robert Atkins's direction it had a more satisfactory representation. Gatty, like Rutland Boughton, belonged to the generation which could not escape being influenced by Wagner, but in both these cases the native English influences were still stronger. In Gatty's opera there were happy reminiscences of Purcell, and it could be said that while the villains of his drama sang in something like the language of Bayreuth, Ariel and the spirits of the masque floated in the ethereal atmosphere of *King Arthur* and *The Fairy Queen*.

Another opera by Nicholas Gatty which was for a long time very popular at the Vic was *Prince Ferelon*, called by its composer an 'extravaganza'. It was peculiarly well suited to the opera audience of the Vic in those days, for that audience seemed to have a certain homogeneity as well as a certain consciousness of intimate under-standing with those on the stage. As long as the opera was confined to the Lambeth theatre, the audience remained more or less the same; newcomers were always being welcomed, but they were immediately absorbed into 'the family', and the opera singers, ever since the production of *Figaro*, had subconsciously developed a sense of ensemble that was not confined to the actual performance of concerted numbers in Mozart. *Prince Ferelon* had a certain rather child-like directness and simplicity, a certain *amateurishness*, if I may be allowed to use the word in its best possible sense without the faintest trace of disparagement, and the same quality was observable in Ethel Smyth's amusing opera *The Bo'sun's Mate*, which at once went to the hearts of the Old Vic audience. At Covent Garden, or at any other West End theatre where operatic experiments were tried, the audience would have been too sophisticated for these little entertainments, too anxious to keep up their reputation for connoisseur-ship. At the Vic, both operas were extremely well sung, as an actual matter of fact, but that did not seem to matter; the operas were *enjoyed*, the audience laughed and it was all great fun. When the opera department moved into Sadler's Wells Gatty and Ethel Smyth, like Balfe and Wallace, were left behind; the audience at Sadler's Wells was an utterly unknown quantity, and even down to the outbreak of war and the closing of the theatre in 1941 there was no such homogeneity at Sadler's Wells as there had been in Lambeth, even though the theatre might be full night after night and the audience genuinely enthusiastic.

But I must go back for a moment to 1920, for in that year Rutland Boughton brought his singers and dancers from Glastonbury to give a few performances at the Old Vic. The story of the Glastonbury Festivals is outside the scope of this book, but their momentary contact with London at the Vic gave the impulse to a wider appreciation of Boughton's aims and achievements. The conventional operatic world had naturally nothing but ridicule and contempt for a crazy visionary who was setting up to create 'an English Bayreuth' in a Somersetshire village, with a disused schoolroom for theatre, a very much disused grand pianoforte for orchestra, and human beings waving their arms or standing in motionless poses in lieu of scenery as a background to a tetralogy about King Arthur and the Round Table. Those who took the trouble to make the journey to Glastonbury came home with very different impressions. It was not in the least true that Boughton had started his Festivals to perform his own works; it was not even true that Wagner intended Bayreuth to be limited to his own works. But whatever differences of opinion there might be about the Arthurian cycle – on which nobody can really form an adequate judgment until it is performed in a proper theatre with all the scenic and orchestral resources that it demands – there was no doubt that two works of unmistakable originality and practical stage effectiveness had come out of Glastonbury – *The Immortal Hour* and the Christmas mystery-opera, if I may so call it, *Bethlehem*. Whenever Sadler's Wells is reopened permanently, or if the company finds a permanent home in any other theatre, these two works ought to belong to its regular repertory. In 1920 the Old Vic was the only theatre in London where they could find the right audience; at the Vic there was understanding for them from the first.

In 1923 the London County Council insisted on a drastic reconstruction of the theatre, and this was carried out in 1924 with funds mainly supplied by the generosity of Sir George Dance. A new site was found for Morley College, and the whole of the Victoria building now became available for the purposes of opera and drama. Although opera was still limited to two days a week, the repertory was being steadily developed. Geoffrey Toye and Percy Pitt had both joined the Board of Governors, and their specialised knowledge and experience were of great value to the musical work of the theatre. Corri was beginning to show signs of failing health, and on one or two occasions Toye or Pitt had to take his place at the conductor's desk at rather short notice. Verdi's *Otello* was performed for the first time at the Vic in April 1928; it was a truly remarkable achievement, and it further had the advantage of some striking scenery designed by E. McKnight Kauffer for Shakespeare's play. Unfortunately, it was found that the Shakespearean scenery was not really very suitable for the opera, as it left little room for the chorus. *Tosca* and *Hänsel and Gretel* were also added to the repertory about this time, and the last-named opera has remained an eternal favourite for Christmas holiday audiences.

In January, 1931, Sadler's Wells Theatre was at last reopened as an 'Old Vic for North London'. After the tenancy of Phelps came to an end in 1862 the reputation of Sadler's Wells gradually declined. It relapsed into being a suburban melodrama house; later it became a music hall (1893-1913). Once again it tried melodrama twice nightly; in 1914 it was a cinema and in 1915 it was closed altogether and left to become derelict. The chief initiator and dauntless organiser of the scheme for its rescue, recovery and rebuilding was the late Sir Reginald Rowe. The present theatre incorporates part of the original exterior walls but not more; the interior was planned on modern lines so as to accommodate 1,650 spectators and to give every single one of them a really good view of the stage. The measurements of the stage itself were almost identical with those of the Vic, so that scenery could be used interchangeably at both theatres without inconvenience.

The original idea was to perform drama and opera for alternate weeks at each theatre, and the principle of alternation was kept up for two years; but it gradually became evident that the system was unworkable in practice. The alternate weeks became alternate months, and finally it was decided by the Governors that Drama and Opera must be completely separated, Drama being housed at the Old Vic and Opera at the Wells. The local public of Islington and Finsbury were evidently quite unprepared for Shakespeare and serious drama; from the first it became apparent that opera was more likely to fill the house. It was right that the experiment should be tried of performing both, but as soon as the experiment led to a definite conclusion it was obviously right to face the situation. In any case, Sadler's Wells was a risky experiment and a costly one too; there was a deficit of over £3,000 on the first year's workings. The second year showed slightly better results, but there was still a deficit, and for the rest of Miss Baylis's lifetime Sadler's Wells was a cause of chronic financial anxiety.

From the first opening of the new theatre it was clear that opera could no longer be carried on there according to the old-fashioned system of the Vic. Corri realised at once that his own reign was over, and he yielded up his baton willingly and generously to Lawrance Collingwood who for so many years had served him faithfully and laboriously in various humble capacities at the Vic. The Vic opera was Corri's creation, and he told Collingwood plainly that Sadler's Wells would have to be built up by his successor. Miss Baylis herself was utterly unprepared for the new developments which the opening of Sadler's Wells inevitably involved. When the first announcement was made to the Governors that there would be alternate weeks of opera and drama, I said myself, 'Then I suppose that means that we shall now have opera every night of the week for eight months'. (The theatres were both of them closed for one night weekly, but with the inclusion of matinées there would be at least six performances a week.)

Lord Lytton, the chairman, put the question to Miss Baylis. She seemed completely taken by surprise. 'Yes, I suppose there will', she replied with a rather dazed look, as if it had never occurred to her that the whole work of the opera department would from now onwards be doubled if not more. That meant too that we should require more singers, producers and conductors, as well as more expenditure on scenery and other accessories. The opening of Sadler's Wells at once increased the work of both theatres, and put them completely on the level of a national playhouse

1 *Sadler's Wells Theatre, 1720.* 2 *Aquatic Theatre, Sadler's Wells, 1813.* 3 *Sadler's Wells Theatre, 1880.*

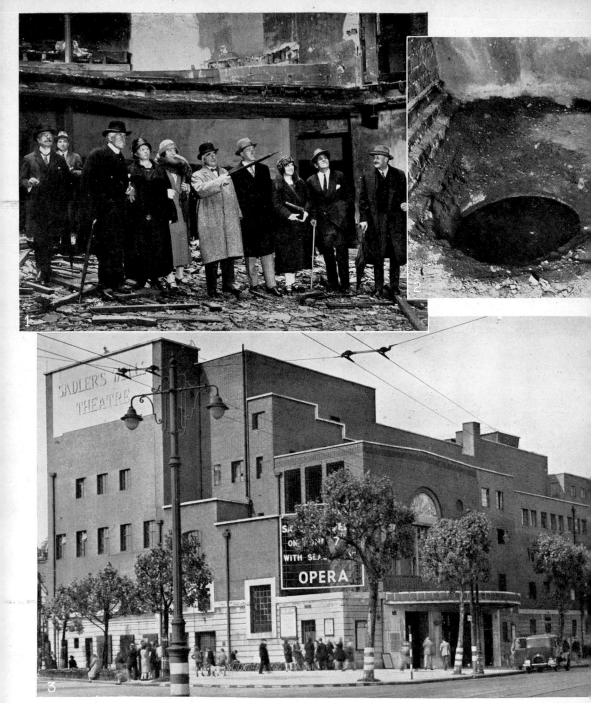

1 *Demolition of old Sadler's Wells Theatre.* Group, left to right: *Squire Bancroft, Lilian Baylis, Edith Evans, Sir Arthur Pinero, Matheson Lang, Mrs. Matheson Lang, Balliol Holloway, Sir Reginald Rowe.* **2** *The Well.* **3** *Sadler's Wells Theatre — Re-opening, June 7th, 1945.* [*Photo: Angus McBean.*]

and opera house. At both theatres the artistic directors and all concerned rose to their new responsibilities. It was felt at once that on the opera side operas must be adequately rehearsed and staged, and that the orchestra must be increased to something like what the composers had indicated in their scores.

The minute-books of the Governors' Board show that there were recurrent complaints from Governors about the inadequacy with which the operas were presented. As far back as 1920 Adrian Boult, at that time a Governor, was protesting against the lack of proper rehearsal; in later years Lady Gooch and others continued to demand improvement and a higher standard altogether. To all these criticisms Miss Baylis had one and the same answer, an answer that was indeed irrefutable; more rehearsals meant the expenditure of more money, and they simply could not be afforded. The Musicians' Union has always treated the Old Vic and Sadler's Wells in a very forbearing and generous spirit, but orchestral players must live, and it was inevitable that they should combine to raise their fees when all living expenses were rising. The prices of admission to the Vic and Wells had inevitably to be raised too, and stalls which in the days before 1914 had cost two shillings gradually came to cost six or even seven. The most rigid economy had to be practised with regard to scenery and costumes. It was an age when economy was the dominating factor in theatrical production in every theatre of Europe. In some countries the problem was solved by new and daring experiments in symbolism; but after much experience of trial and error, the leading opera houses gradually came to the conclusion that for some reason opera could not be staged in the same 'expressionist' technique as drama or even ballet.

Critics of an older age, such as Schlegel in Germany and Hazlitt, following him in England, used to regard sumptuousness and magnificence as indispensable qualities of the opera; they had inherited the traditions of dynastic and baroque opera in the seventeenth century, traditions which the romantic movement never swept away, least of all in Italy, so that up to the present day, or as near that as we can estimate, the Scala at Milan still mounted its operas with the photographic realism of a coloured picture postcard, and with all those architectural grandiosities which for half a century or more have been characteristic of Italian hotels and railway stations. At Sadler's Wells such effects would always have been impossible owing to the restricted proportions of the stage. The whole theatre was built in a style of aggressive austerity and contrasted strangely with the picturesquely faded grandeurs of the Vic as it was in 1920. The drab colouring and the peculiar angles of the proscenium walls do not lead the eye happily towards the stage picture; the gilded shields above and the two marble staircases rising up from the orchestra below are unpleasant distractions. The stage always seems to be too near for the effects of

G

Wagnerian romance and too far for the intimacy of Mozartian comedy. At the Vic one was never offended by the shabbiness of the scenery; the rather dilapidated conventional sets seemed to belong naturally to a rather dilapidated and conventional theatre. At Sadler's Wells necessity was never very prolific of invention, and in many operas the wilful abstention from grandeur, the elevation of economy into a moral principle – 'oh, but it's so old-fashioned to be realistic! We leave all these things to the imagination now' – was depressing in the extreme. Lohengrin was not allowed to have a swan at all; the swan was 'suggested' by a light which looked as if the operator had intended to 'spot' the hero himself but always missed him; *Carmen* and *Orpheus* were other operas which were definitely painful to look upon. One could have felt sentimental at least over decorations that were old-fashioned and shabby; but the combination of newness and cheapness was unpleasant. On the other hand, a few of the new operas achieved strikingly successful pictures, notably the Russian works; Collingwood was a great enthusiast for Russian opera in all forms and whenever a Russian opera was put on it was an outstanding event in every way. Any opera

house in Europe might have been proud of Rimsky-Korsakov's *Snow Maiden*, the same composer's *Tsar Saltan*, and Mussorgsky's *Boris Godunov* in the original unretouched version – all three first performances in England. There was also a very sensitive and understanding production of *Eugene Onegin*.

Miss Baylis herself viewed all these experiments with more anxiety than pride. Would they fill the house? If they did not fill it to capacity for the second and third performances they were taken off at once and regarded as hopeless failures. Some operas filled the gallery but not the stalls; *Eugene Onegin* filled the stalls but not the gallery. She began to feel that the opera – the thing that she really loved the most – was getting beyond her own intellectual powers. It took me ten years of persistent nagging to get her to produce *Fidelio*. 'I'm an ignorant woman,' she said. 'I don't know anything about *Fidelio;* I've never seen it; I only know it's always been a failure at Covent Garden.' 'Just the very reason why *we* ought to make it a success,' I rejoined. It was Miss Gough's gentle persuasion that finally induced her to agree to it. One would think that she might have asked Collingwood to play the opera through to her with a few of the singers to give her an idea of it; but probably she had no time for that. The terror of debt was always on her mind; there was never enough money for anything. This was no delusion on her part; it was just the naked truth, and that was why both theatres were perpetually understaffed, the performers underpaid, and the operas under-rehearsed. Sadler's Wells could just have kept its head above water if it had been sold out for every single performance. Other managers, such as Schikaneder in Mozart's days, running a theatre very like the Old Vic, sometimes had the courage to go on and on with a play or opera, in spite of poor houses to begin with, until the public got into the habit of going to it and ultimately made it into a success. When *Lilac Time* was first put on the stage in England, I went to the third performance of it and found myself almost alone in the pit. Miss Baylis could not afford to have courage or perseverance on behalf of doubtful successes. I cannot blame her for taking a great many operas off after three nights; but that is no reason why they should be regarded as failures for ever and ever, and several of these discarded works might well be staged again. Indeed, the experiment has been tried only recently. Smetana's *The Bartered Bride* was a complete failure when first produced at Sadler's Wells; revived in 1944 at the New Theatre and produced by a Czech ballet-master with a really efficient ballet, it has proved brilliantly successful both in London and in the provinces.

The trouble with practically all conductors in all countries is that they are very seldom interested in voices or in what is going on on the stage. They all want to conduct huge orchestras, all the more so if they are not allowed much time for rehearsal. There is sound reason for this; modern orchestral players are completely at their ease in Wagner and Richard Strauss, so that they can be pretty safely trusted to play through any of their operas without a conductor at all. And even if some instruments do go astray, the chances are that very few members of an operatic audience will notice it, since their attention is a good deal distracted by the stage. On the other hand, operas by older composers, utilising a smaller orchestra and preferring in general a much thinner instrumental texture, are often very troublesome to rehearse, since an exact balance must be obtained in combinations of instruments that are now out of fashion and in many cases the music refuses to 'play itself' like Wagner and requires really imaginative interpretation.

It certainly was a remarkable achievement on the part of Sadler's Wells to stage *The Mastersingers* and *The Valkyrie*, and perhaps an even more astonishing *tour de force* to present a thoroughly convincing performance of *Der Rosenkavalier*, convincing in every department, for it was thoroughly well sung and acted with great spirit; if the scenery was not so magnificent as that of Dresden it was at any rate well designed and effective in a comparatively small theatre. Whether these ambitions, certainly laudable in isolated cases, and indeed justified by success, were really the right course for Sadler's Wells to pursue at that moment may be doubted. Expenses mounted steadily and it could never be satisfactory from the economic point of view to make a regular practice of mounting costly operas for which even a completely full house could never pay.

Much more important, though perhaps not so thoroughly appreciated by the audiences of the moment, were the various operas by British composers which were brought forward during the Sadler's Wells period. First, by right of antiquity, Purcell's *Dido and Aeneas*, conducted by Constant Lambert, whose essentially scholarly imagination seized all its dramatic points. Ever since the bicentenary of Purcell's death in 1895 *Dido and Aeneas* has had an increasing number of amateur performances. It was composed for a girls' school and it is eminently suitable for a school opera performance; at first it was generally given in concert form, but latterly there has been more and more of a tendency to put it on the stage. The professional opera companies ignored it completely. At Sadler's Wells it received the recognition due to a great national classic, and once a certain professional standard of performance had been set, it could be revived again from time to time, as it was quite recently, as a regular item of the standard repertory. The other opera by a deceased British master was Stanford's *The Travelling Companion*. Sadler's Wells was by no means the first in the field with this work. The score had been published in 1919, but Stanford did not live to see it on the stage; he died in 1924. A year later it was given for the first time by amateurs at Liverpool; next at Bristol during a short opera festival organised by the late P. Napier Miles in the old Theatre Royal in October 1926. Miss Radford revived it at Falmouth with her amateur company (which had already given a whole series of interesting opera performances) in 1934 and it was only in March 1935 that Sadler's Wells had the courage to present it in London. The company were deeply impressed with it, and enjoyed singing in it, with a certain sense of devotion not often experienced in the general routine of operatic work; if the financial situation had allowed it to be kept on the stage for a certain period at a loss, it would probably have established itself quite definitely in popular favour, for its audiences were at any rate increasing, though not fast enough for Miss Baylis's anxious eye.

Collingwood's *Macbeth* met a similar fate; it was a very distinguished piece of work and ought certainly to be put on the stage again as soon as more settled conditions prevail; the same may be said of Nicholas Gatty's *Greysteel*. The most successful of the British operas was undoubtedly *Hugh the Drover*, by Ralph Vaughan Williams, and as the composer intended, it made the chorus almost the principal character of the drama, a task to which the Sadler's Wells chorus responded with magnificent enthusiasm. Another opera of Vaughan Williams also made a momentary appearance at Sadler's Wells – *The Poisoned Kiss*, which had had its first production at Cambridge, mainly by amateurs; the Cambridge company repeated it in London at the end of the normal Sadler's Wells season. Lastly we must mention *The Wreckers*, by Ethel Smyth. Her own story of her career as an opera composer, with all her struggles and disappointments from 1898 onwards, must be read in her own words. It does not matter whether she was really a great composer or not, nor does it matter that she was a woman and had, or thought she had, all sorts of sex-prejudices to contend

Dame Ethel
her dog. Pan
& her listening
apparatus

with. The same fate might have befallen any male composer; Ethel Smyth's auto-biography – dispersed through various books of hers, and all enthralling to read – is a chapter of general social and operatic history. *The Wreckers* had been composed as a French opera, *Les Naufrageurs*, the composer knowing at that time that she had no chance of a performance in England. It was first produced in German, at Leipzig in 1906, and in the same year given at the German opera house in Prague. Beecham gave the first English performance in 1909; no other manager would ever have had either the courage or the imagination to consider it. After thirty years it was revived by Sadler's Wells, and the venerable composer, so much afflicted by deafness that she could not hear a note of it, watched the performance from a seat in the auditorium and was hailed with affectionate acclamations at the end.

BY THE end of Queen Victoria's reign the art of ballet in this country had sunk to an almost negligible position. There were always plenty of English dancers, of course, but the general idea of ballet as an organised art was that it belonged either to the Italian Opera and was definitely an importation from abroad, either from Italy or France, or to Christmas pantomime and entertainments of a more or less frivolous character. A few teachers still kept up quite a high level of physical technique, notably Madame Katti Lanner (1831-1908), the daughter of Josef Lanner, famous as the creator of the Viennese waltz. Katti Lanner was responsible for most of the dancers who appeared in pantomimes and especially in the long series of ballets which were brought out at the Empire Theatre in Leicester Square; her style was, of course, strictly classical, for she had been trained in Vienna and had danced there in the days of Fanny Elssler, Taglioni and Cerito. No doubt there were a number of *balletomanes*, as they are now called, who frequented the Empire and posed as connoisseurs, but during the nineteenth century ballet in general had become slightly disreputable from the moral point of view, not only in London but still more in Paris and Vienna, so that the *habitués* of the ballet were mostly gentlemen of pleasure. A character in Frank Smedley's novel *Lewis Arundel* (1852) describes the ballet at the Italian Opera as 'a set of jumping Jezebels, skipping about in white muslin kilts, for they're nothing better; respectable people ought to be ashamed of looking at 'em'. No dancer in those days was ever expected to be able to live on her wages from the theatre.

In the early years of the present century a reaction set in, headed by Isadora Duncan, whose aim was to restore the natural grace of ancient Greek dancing. She trained many pupils and had an enormous following, especially in Germany, where the 'philosophical' aspect of her system was keenly appreciated and eagerly pursued. In England her influence – passed on through various pupils and imitators – hardly affected the professional stage at all, but her methods were widely adopted among amateurs, that is, for the elementary training of quite small children and for the further development of adolescents. Here her style made contact with the ideas of Monsieur Jaques-Dalcroze on the educational values of music and rhythm. The training which he called 'eurhythmics' would hardly have been possible without the preliminary work of Isadora Duncan and various other teachers and theorists, some of them interested as much in classical archæology as in modern music. Almost simultaneously there arose in England the cult of collecting traditional folk-dances and reproducing them. Here again the primary impulse was educational rather than artistic. Mary Neal started the folk-dance movement with the 'Esperance' girls' club; she was like Miss Cons in a way, as her fundamental interests were in social welfare work in the East End. Mary Neal was certainly the first pioneer in modern folk-dancing long before Cecil Sharp was ever heard of. But she was quite unscientific and had no interest in the archæology of folk-dancing; folk-dances to her were merely a means of bringing a new kind of happiness into the life of slum children – a bunch of wild flowers from the country and no more. Cecil Sharp was

"Ballet had become slightly disreputable"
(Rake's Progress)

more of a researcher and 'folklorist', though not really a man of scholarship; he was rather more like a practical bird-watcher and field naturalist than a scientific zoologist.

These movements are mentioned here because they were very characteristically English; they appealed primarily to amateurs, and as far as their dance value was concerned, it was almost exclusively moral and educational. On the professional stage Cecil Sharp had even less influence than Isadora Duncan. If anyone attempted to utilise the steps of folk-dances and adapt them freely for dramatic purposes, such as a dance or masque in a play, Cecil Sharp was up in arms at once against the profanation of things that to him and his inner ring of disciples were holy and untouchable. They wanted to see folk-dancing spread all over England, over the Empire and the English-speaking world, as indeed it has done; but they did not want to see it as a ballet in the theatre. Experiments were tried by ingenious choreographers; but the general verdict was that for ballet purposes English folk-dances were no good.

On the Continent Isadora Duncan was taken more seriously, though the consequences of her stimulus were sometimes grotesque. Du Maurier's novel *Trilby* had become famous all over Europe, and a successor to Svengali appeared in Munich where a certain Madame Madeleine, as she was called, appeared on the stage ostensibly under the hypnotic influence of a doctor – let me call him Dr. Mirakel, as I have forgotten his name. The lady was supposed to go into a trance, and in this condition she 'interpreted' various pieces of music such as Chopin's *Marche Funèbre*, Rubinstein's *Spring Song* and other favourite classics. The alleged hypnosis launched her into a momentary fame; even in Germany she is no longer remembered. But what was remembered and what was imitated and developed into something like a genuine work of art was the principle of interpreting a piece of classical music in dance and gesture. The music of the old-fashioned classical ballet was always trivial. Délibes and Tchaikovsky were not typical ballet-composers; they were rare exceptions of genius. The typical ballet of those days was Marenco's *Excelsior*, a string of commonplace waltzes, polkas and galops, now hardly known except in military band selections. Another point worth mentioning in connection with Madame Madeleine was that she started the solo dance recital with a pianoforte accompaniment. In later years this type of solo recital was to be seen all over Germany; in England it never took root. There are no suitable places for it in London, except perhaps the Mercury Theatre. Most theatres are much too large (and their rents too high) and the smaller halls for concerts have no facilities for even the simplest effects of stage lighting and decoration.

When the Russian Ballet first came to Paris in 1909 they stopped in Berlin on their way. For Berlin, as for Paris, they were something entirely new, and it may surprise the English reader to learn that they were at once seized upon by the painters of the Berlin *Secession*, that is, by those who were then considered the ultra-modernists, the imitators of the French Impressionists and one or two who had even got as far as Post-Impressionism. At first sight it seemed incredible that painters of that type, violently opposed to all that was orthodox and conventional, should ally themselves with the ultra-conventional ballet of the Russians. What the painters saw at once and honoured was their colossal technical skill. They also appreciated the fact that the Russian theatre employed the finest artists of the country to design scenery and costumes, whereas in those days the court theatres of Germany depended on scene painters of no originality or imagination – such gifts indeed would have been severely disapproved of by the high-born directors of these establishments.

In Germany the Russian drama had more influence on the theatre than the Russian Ballet. The ballet came and went, and after the end of the war in 1918 the ballet was more at home in Paris and Monte Carlo than in Berlin. The Russian theatre, performing plays in Russian, often with marvellous scenery and costumes for pieces of a historical type, certainly left its mark on Max Reinhardt. In London, after the war was over and the arts were free to flourish once more, the admirers of the Russians were divided more or less into two camps – those who worshipped the one and only Anna Pavlova, with a perceptible share of adoration for her male partner Michael Mordkin, and the followers of Serge Diaghilev. Pavlova represented the extreme individualism of the solo performer, Diaghilev stood for the suppression of personal temperament and the perfection of technique and ensemble. Massine said to me himself in those days – and said it with a noble expression of pride – 'Dans le ballet russe il n'y a pas de solistes'. It is well that this dictum should be remembered, because at this distance of time writers on ballet inevitably tend to recall the individual stars rather than the total achievement. And the total achievement of Diaghilev was indeed so gigantic and so varied in content that it is difficult to sum it up in a few sentences. All his ballets, whether people approved of them or not, were works of art; it did not matter really that some of them might be works of perverse art, typical of various eccentric tendencies in painting or music which flourished briefly in the years that followed the war. However absurd, they were at least 'art for art's sake', and not merely commercial routine. There was technique, accomplishment, mechanical precision, and all at their highest potentials, in the Diaghilev ballet, but never routine. And there was novelty too; music by new composers such as Stravinsky and Prokofiev, decorations by new painters like Picasso and Derain, all brought into an *ensemble* that had never been contemplated in ballet before.

In these days lovers of ballet, whether they belong to the inner ring or only to the outer fringe, are so accustomed to the modern outlook on ballet as an art independent of opera and of all other types of stage entertainment, that they can hardly realise what conditions were like in the old days of the Empire Theatre. The arrival of Adeline Genée in 1897 lifted the Empire ballet on to a higher plane and the standard was maintained for the next ten years, thanks to her singularly captivating personality. She brought a male dancer with her from Copenhagen, and it is curious in these days to note the grudging praise that was given to him by London criticism. 'If a male dancer is bearable at all' – then this gentleman certainly deserved his triumph. It was the tradition in those days that all male parts in ballet should be danced by women, like the 'principal boys' of pantomime, and our one great male dancer, Mr. Vokes, was never expected to appear in any part except the 'demon king'. One of the sensations of that Jubilee year 1897 was an Empire ballet composed by Sullivan, *Victoria and*

Merrie England; I cannot imagine Sadler's Wells ever attempting to revive it, although in those days it was much respected by the musical critics because it included a danced fugue.* That was long before Dalcroze's pupils danced the fugues of Bach as part of their normal routine training. Milan was a great centre of ballet in those remote days, and it was there that *Excelsior* was produced in 1881. It was one of the numerous hymns to progress inspired by Longfellow and had been planned as far back as 1877 under the very title of *Progresso.* The music was by Romualdo Marenco; the choreographer was Luigi Manzotti. The story, like those of all the pantomimes in England, is conducted by *compère* and *commère*, demon king and fairy queen, here called Spirit of Obscurantism and Spirit of Progress. Volta sees his electric pile destroyed as an instrument of sorcery; the fairy queen shows him a vision of the Post Office at Washington and a ballet of telegraph boys. Papin is lynched for unfairly winning a university boatrace with his steamboat against an oar-driven eight; we are transported to the Hudson with liners arriving and trains rushing across Brooklyn Bridge. The Suez Canal is opened, the Mont Cenis tunnel pierced and the evening ends with a grand ballet of all nations. *Excelsior* still lives, or did so until recently, in Italy; many times have I heard the music in the Piazza at Venice, and I have seen the whole ballet staged at Florence, as well as at the little marionette theatre in Milan, where it seemed more at home than anywhere else.

Diaghilev too had some idea of a 'ballet of all nations'. The Russian revolution drove him and his dancers out of Russia, and they made their chief home at Monte Carlo; it was a significant symbol of Diaghilev's personality, standing for internationalism and exclusiveness at the same time, 'luxe, calme et volupté' as Baudelaire put it. They went to Spain and picked up the *Cuadro flamenco*, a genuine troupe of Spanish dancers and singers – Spain had just begun to be fashionable among the intellectuals who had exhausted Italy, even the baroque extravagances of Sicily and Apulia; they staged their own ancient Russian folklore and the latest eccentricities from Paris. On one occasion Diaghilev risked a magnificent revival of Tchaikovsky's *The Sleeping Beauty*, one of the old Russian court ballets that filled an entire evening. London was not ripe for that; it demanded too much concentration on the great historic traditions of choreography, and the ordinary public found it as dreary as an oratorio. The influence of the Russian Ballet, as we can now see, made itself felt gradually all over Europe; neither Germany nor Italy accepted it whole-heartedly, but it was a force that had to be reckoned with. Italy reverted to her ancient routine; that was

* 'The other day, when I was in Gibraltar, I witnessed the arrival of some of the befeathered "Australian contingent" [i.e. the Australian cavalry who figured in the Jubilee procession]; they were splendid fellows, who looked as if the world belonged, and ought to belong, to them. On the Alhambra stage they are ladies with waists, and the music that attends them is also a lady with a waist.' (Robert Hichens, in *The Musician*, June 2, 1897.)

always a safe investment. Germany philosophised and discussed, and some interesting attempts were made to put the Diaghilev ballets on the German stage. I saw performances of *Pétrouchka* at Cologne and Hanover, both got up by conductors who had never heard the music played and by choreographers who had never seen the ballet anywhere; *Pulcinella* was given at Hanover too. The London *balletomanes*, guardians of the sacred traditions, would no doubt have been horrified; I could only

A POPULAR BELIEF: LIFE WITH THE BALLETS RUSSES.

marvel at the extraordinary accomplishment of sheer imagination and what a musician would call 'score-reading ability'.

Diaghilev died in 1929, and as in the case of Miss Baylis, most people in the outside world said that the whole conception of Russian Ballet would die with him. This was a true prophecy in so far as Diaghilev himself was a personality that could never be exactly reproduced; but the main principles for which he stood still held good, and although the title of 'Ballets Russes' was appropriated by another company operating under Russian direction and including a certain number of genuine Russians among its choreographers and dancers, it is safe to say that the company which has interpreted Diaghilev's ideals most consistently and which has shown too that they could be carried to a further development is that of Sadler's Wells. Other companies may claim to have inherited 'the traditions' and the performing rights in some of Diaghilev's most successful ballets; Sadler's Wells is far too vital to live on relics of the past – it has no need of traditions, because it is always creating something new.

Ninette de Valois, as she chose to call herself, came from Ireland and joined Diaghilev's company in 1924, but remained with him for two years only. After that she opened a ballet school of her own and also helped in the direction of the Abbey Theatre in Dublin and the Festival Theatre at Cambridge. In the latter she was associated with Norman Marshall as producer and Hedley Briggs as actor, dancer and designer; it was in this theatre, too, that Walter Leigh, whose early death deprived British music of 'a second Sullivan', it was said – and indeed deprived it of far more than that – began his experience as a man of the theatre. The Diaghilev of the Festival Theatre was Terence Gray, whose productions aroused the moral indignation of some of the middle-aged ladies of Cambridge, the contemptuous amusement of the orthodox connoisseurs, and the everlasting delight of those who were ready to appreciate and enjoy a fantastic and sometimes outrageous spirit of artistic experiment. Mr. Haskell has said that the chief characteristic of Ninette de Valois was her stubborn determination against what seems at the time to be common sense; if that was not already in her Irish blood, it must have been instilled into her at the Festival Theatre. Her first chance of making a name in London came with the foundation of the Camargo Society in 1930, for which she produced *Job*, 'a masque for dancing' after designs by William Blake. *Job* too had many connections with Cambridge; the idea of it started with Geoffrey Keynes, eminent surgeon and at the same time our greatest living authority on Blake, the scenery and costumes were the work of Gwendolen Raverat, *née* Darwin, and the music by her cousin Ralph Vaughan Williams. He had already composed a ballet *Old King Cole* in 1923, intended mainly for folk-dancers and produced in the open air at Cambridge by amateurs; *Job*, on the other hand, was a profoundly serious and even mystical work. Diaghilev, one may be sure, would have been terrified at it; it would have met with no response at Monte Carlo. Here, it has passed into our classical repertory of ballet – music, designs, choreography and all; and after fourteen years it seems more firmly established in our respect and admiration than many of the composer's works for the concert platform. In July, 1931, it was performed at Oxford as an item in the festival of the International Society for Contemporary Music along with Constant Lambert's *Pomona* and a ballet by the Czech composer Erwin Schulhoff, this last danced by a Czech company; it was the first time that ballet had made its appearance in any of the International Society's festivals.

Miss Baylis had opened Sadler's Wells Theatre in January of that year. She had already employed Ninette de Valois at the Old Vic in 1929 to arrange ballets for Molière's play *The Imaginary Invalid*, and occasionally a little ballet was allowed to precede a short opera such as *Hänsel and Gretel*. The first of her ballets, danced by the regular opera dancers of the Vic, who were volunteers, reinforced by some of Miss de Valois's own pupils from her Academy of Choreographic Art, as it was magnilo-quently called, was Mozart's *Les Petits Riens;* another was *The Picnic* danced to the music of Vaughan Williams's *Charterhouse Suite*. A curious musical play by Clemence Dane, *Adam's Opera*, with music by Richard Addinsell, now known to fame through his *Warsaw Concerto*, also required the help of the ballet. The real *début* of the Sadler's Wells Ballet may be said to date from a gala ballet performance in aid of Queen Charlotte's Hospital in which Lydia Lopokova and Anton Dolin took part; Constant Lambert conducted.

Constant Lambert (b. 1905) was first discovered by Vaughan Williams, under

Constant Lambert
conducting Comus
Anatole

whom he studied composition at the Royal College of Music, and his second dis-
coverer was Diaghilev, who commissioned him to write a ballet, *Romeo and Juliet*,
first performed at Monte Carlo in 1926, followed by *Pomona*, produced at Buenos
Aires in 1927. The modern age has seen many conductors who aspired to be composers, and a few composers who were interested in conducting works not their
own; Constant Lambert is one of the rare few who have attained real eminence in
both capacities. When we add that he is a learned researcher and a witty and pene-
trating writer of musical criticism as well, it can be understood what immensely
valuable gifts he brought to the Sadler's Wells Ballet by his immediate and lasting

The pooled resources of contemporary music (interpreted from Constant Lambert's book 'Music Ho!').

association with Ninette de Valois. Diaghilev had employed all the most distinguished composers that he could discover, but none of them ever faced the daily drudgery of accompanying at the pianoforte, rehearsing and conducting an orchestra night after night. This has been Lambert's regular work since 1931; it has given him a unique position among conductors and composers, but far more important than that is the contribution of this experience to the development of British ballet. The Sadler's Wells Ballet achieved popularity from its first night, and very soon it had filled the house so successfully that the Governors were only too happy to increase the number of its weekly performances, since it provided a happy compensation for the losses incurred by the operas. In the early years the Ballet took part in the operas as well, and *Faust* with Gounod's complete ballet music was one of the attractions of the repertory.

The ballet group, however, as was only natural, were more interested in pursuing an independent course. In Continental theatres it was quite usual for a programme to contain a triple bill of two small operas and a ballet, or two ballets and an opera; at Sadler's Wells this was always regarded as out of the question. The public had apparently made up its mind that it would not tolerate triple bills or one-act operas of any kind, except the invariable *Cavalleria* and *Pagliacci*, which were regarded as inseparable, as if they were two acts of the same opera. The consequence was that the opera and the ballet became as complete strangers to one another as the opera and the drama had been at the Vic. The ballet required fewer orchestral players and brought larger audiences; it also had supporters like the Camargo Society and the Sadler's Wells Society which were able and willing to find money for new dresses and scenery by distinguished artists – whereas the orchestral demands of the opera combined with its precarious audiences were a cause of eternal worry and anxiety to Miss Baylis.

The opera was obliged to play for safety and stick to the orthodox repertory; *Boris Godunov* was its only approach to real modernity in style, although that opera dated from 1870. The ballet throve on modernity; from a purely musical point of view its influence has been of great educational value, for through this means audiences which perhaps do not frequent concerts of modern music have been gradually and agreeably made aware of the new tendencies. Lambert has had a free hand and has pursued a consistent and practical policy. Whenever he has the chance of conducting an ordinary symphony concert you may be sure that he will draw up no ordinary programme. He is certain to avoid all the hackneyed classics and the hackneyed 'popular' items too; but his knowledge of all music is so far-reaching that he can always think of unusual works, seldom heard in the ordinary routine concerts, some of them modern, others almost 'museum pieces', but all of them made attractive and convincing by his scholarly and imaginative interpretation. How the new ballets are evolved I have not the slightest idea, but in some cases I can imagine him playing a selection of unfamiliar pieces by Liszt to Miss de Valois and saying 'you might make a romantic ballet out of that'; or at another time she might say to him 'I think Milton's *Comus* would make a good ballet', and he would immediately say, 'Yes, and we must have music by Purcell for it'. A blind man might go to the ballet any night and always be certain of listening to a programme of really good music.

It is this close co-operation of three arts, all on the highest level of achievement, that has given the Sadler's Wells Ballet its peculiar character, for what I have said about the music applies no less to the *décor* and the choreography, all of which, especially in combination, are really of far greater importance than the virtuosity of individual solo dancers. And it has really been very fortunate that the Sadler's Wells company turned its back from the first on almost the entire Diaghilev repertory.

In spite of the doctrine that there were no soloists in the Russian Ballet the famous ballets of those years were inevitably associated in the memories of the connoisseurs with certain individuals. Besides that, many of the ballets were copyright properties and therefore definitely not available to the new organisation. Miss de Valois and her various choreographers had to draw upon their own originality, and the result has been a long series of ballets, mostly short, displaying a wonderful variety of styles. There was a certain basis of what might be called standard classics of ballet, most of them tackled only at a later stage, after the new organisation had completely found its feet: *Sylphides*, popular from the beginning largely, I think, because of its familiar Chopin music, *Casse-Noisette*, which had the same sort of advantage, *Coppélia*, yet another work known to most people by its music alone. It was only after popular audiences had become well educated in appreciation that such long ballets as *Giselle*, *The Swan Lake* and *The Sleeping Beauty* could be presented to them. These are ballets for the connoisseurs who can reel off all the technical terms in Mr. Haskell's glossary; to a mere ignorant enjoyer of ballet like myself there is much more pleasure to be derived from the new ballets that are specifically English in character. I do not want to enlarge upon this essential Englishness, if indeed it exists at all; I have little use for the art which deliberately sets out to be national, so national that its patriotism becomes merely an artificial dressing-up. I suppose that most people would consider *Job* to be the most intensely English of all our ballets; but to me it seems the nearest approach in spirit which Sadler's Wells has made to the German school exemplified by the Ballets Jooss – any German, I think, would say at once that it was *Faustisch*, and it is certainly a good example of what German dancers twenty years ago used to call *kultische Kunst*, hieratic and mystical art.

1 *Robert Helpmann and Pearl Argyle.* [*Photo: J. W. Debenham.*] **2** *Scene in Dressing Room.* [*Photo: Angus McBean.*] **3** *Scene from* Casse Noisette. [*Photo: G. B. L. Wilson.*] **4** *Scene from* Job. [*Photo: J. W. Debenham.*] **5** *The Ballroom Scene,* Apparitions.

[*Photo: J. W. Debenham.*]

1 *and* 2 *Scenes from* The Rake's Progress. *[Photos. Tunbridge-Sedgwick.]* 3 *and* 4 *Scenes from* A Wedding Bouquet. *[Photos: Tunbridge-Sedgwick.]* 5 *Alicia Markova and Anton Dolin.* *[Photo: J. W. Debenham.]* 6 *and* 7 *Scenes from* Giselle *with Margot Fonteyn and Robert Helpmann.* *[Photo: G. B. L. Wilson.]*

Horoscope and Dante Sonata have the same quality of 'other-worldliness'; Checkmate, by Arthur Bliss, was the greatest achievement of the 'English' Ballet after Job, for it had a real sense of tragic grandeur. Jooss on the other hand has resolutely pursued the path of tragedy in ballet, tragedy too with an ethical background that is the inevitable result of all that happened in Germany from 1918 onwards. Big City,

Coppelia

The Birds:
The Dove

Façade:
the Dago

The Green Table, and Pandora all really tell much the same story of the suffering poor, the cruelties of life, the vileness of the profiteer and the pure-mindedness of a proletarian Tamino and Pamina. It is amusing to see how the proletarian theatre which Miss Cons and Miss Baylis thought they were creating has brought forth a type of ballet which is anything but proletarian in its appeal – not indeed a ballet for the aristocracy of imperial Moscow, but certainly for the intellectuals of Bloomsbury.

H

Its ballets have never been naïve or simple-minded; if there was a trace of ethical intent in any of the ballets that I have mentioned, it was hidden behind a mask of artistic scholarship. *Job* has to be approached through a knowledge of Blake, *The Rake's Progress* through Hogarth, and *Dante* through the designs of Flaxman. It is this spirit that awakens my most ardent admiration for the work of Constant Lambert and Ninette de Valois, with whose names it would be only just to couple some of their decorators, notably Oliver Messel. I recognise and admit the seriousness of intention, honour it too, but honour still more intensely their determination to be beautiful before they are good. *Comus* was indeed an experience never to be forgotten: the nobility of the scenic background, the crystalline beauty of Purcell's music, retouched here and there, but only with the exquisite discretion of a true scholar; then the Botticellian elegance and grace of the Lady and – unexpected stroke of genius – the irruption of some thirty or forty lines of the poet himself into the silence of the ballet. And these were all things that could never by any possibility have entered into the imagination of Diaghilev, still less into the minds of his residuary legatees. Purcell, Milton – yes, we English people know all about these – but had we ever before had the inspiration to translate them into the language of ballet?

Apparitions, with music by Liszt, *The Haunted Ballroom* (Geoffrey Toye) and *Hamlet* (Tchaikovsky) were all studies in the macabre; they were also ballets which brought the romantic male dancer into prominence as the central figure of the story. They may also be regarded as stages in the development of Robert Helpmann's individuality. He made his first really powerful impression in *Job*, where he succeeded to the part of Satan, formerly created by Anton Dolin. A little later he appeared as Oberon in *A Midsummer Night's Dream*, a part ideally suited to one who brought to it the remoteness of the ballet-dancer along with an admirable declamation of Shakespeare's poetry. The next step is *Comus* as a ballet, in which Comus is both dancer and actor; even without the spoken words the part depended on miming as well as pure dancing. To make a dancer recite poetry in the middle of a ballet was another thing that might well have frightened Diaghilev; thinking always internationally with Monte Carlo as a background, he would have asked, 'But what language can he recite in, even if he is a good speaker? Russian? Nobody will understand him; French? the Parisians will make fun of his accent; English? Impossible! The English are the last people who want to hear their own language associated with music and dancing'. The effect of the spoken lines in *Comus* was indeed strange, for the rhythmical values of the poetry dominated the intellectual values of the dramatic significance; it was like a song or a piece of music introduced unexpectedly into a spoken drama. The function of music, generally speaking, is to lift poetry on to a still higher spiritual plane; here, it was poetry that performed that office for music. It was not dramatic in delivery, and that was the marvel of it; it had a certain deliberate coldness of colour, the beauty of words in ordered rhythms, which led us into that magical world in which music and poetry are one – the world of Tasso's *Aminta*.

From *Hamlet* as a ballet it was a natural step to *Hamlet* as a play; but the drama does not belong to this chapter.

the Rake's
Progress:
Dancing Master

Albrecht +
"Giselle"

The modern respect shown to the male dancer is due entirely to the influence of the Russians. In the conventional ballet of Paris and Milan his only function was to support the *prima ballerina*, twirl her round and hoist her up. That is practically all that he has to do in *Les Sylphides*; the learned *balletomanes* may be able to explain every movement of the single gentleman who takes part in it, but to the ordinary spectator his only duty seems to be to stand as a contrasting figure and to lift up the ladies so as to give an apex to a pyramidal group – a choreographic effect which has come into many ballets (and is to be found in every acrobatic family group as well), and which on every occasion provokes the enthusiasm of an audience, all the more when it is enhanced by the pictorial unfolding of immense draperies – a device standardised long ago by the painters for the state portraits of female sovereigns. Diaghilev had an eye for the male dancer; Nijinsky, Massine and Lifar became under his direction as world-famous as Taglioni or Carlotta Grisi, and the dances from Borodin's opera *Prince Igor*, essentially Russian and operatic, were given as separate excerpts to show off the virtuosity of the male *corps de ballet*. It was in the masculine ballet that the 'return to nature' really had a vitalising effect; the best of our own native folk-dances are for men only, and it was only with great reluctance, under pressure of circumstances leading to a shortage of men and a superfluity of women, that Cecil Sharp allowed them to be danced by the other sex. Hungary is another country in which all-male dancing plays a large part in country life; Kodály has made striking use of it in his folksong opera *Háry János*, where the *csárdás* of the Hungarian hussars after their capture of Napoleon at the battle of Milan was a truly magnificent sight in the open-air performances at Szeged.

Noverre certainly intended the male dancer to be on equal terms with the female, and he takes a conspicuous part in all the long romantic ballets of the early nineteenth century, of which *Giselle* seems to be now the sole survivor. But the function of all those interminable dance dramas, many of which are in six acts, was to tell a story; their elaborate synopses may often be found in the opera librettos of the period, for it became the fashion, especially in Italy, to perform a short opera with a long ballet, and that is the reason why so many operas of the Paer-Rossini-Bellini period are in two acts only, in order to give time for a ballet in six. These ballets were not integral items in the opera itself, as in *Robert le Diable* or *Tannhäuser*, but completely independent works. But as they were generally adaptations of some previous opera or popular melodrama, they required a firm basis of mime, and the male dancers in these tended naturally to present themselves as actors in dumb-show more than as virtuoso competitors with the ladies. It must be quite clear to anyone who reads through a number of these synopses that the romantic ballet was performing a function very similar to that of the cinema, especially to the cinema of the silent period, for scenery, transformations and all sorts of minor accessories played a much larger part in these entertainments than they have ever done in those of Diaghilev; in Victorian England all these things eventually found their way into that general ragbag of discarded grandeurs – the English Christmas pantomime. The romantic ballet must have been killed by the rise of a new type of romantic drama (Victor Hugo and Alexandre Dumas) and the new type of late romantic opera exemplified by Meyerbeer, Verdi and early Wagner, in which the ballet was to a certain extent incorporated;

but, of course, when ballet was once more made subsidiary to musical drama the dramatic element in it could never stand up against the far more intensely dramatic interest of the opera itself.

And just as Diaghilev could never have conceived such ballets as *Job* and *Comus*, so he certainly could never have imagined *Façade*, though he might have enjoyed it very much if he had lived to see it. *Façade* presented a new form of humour in ballet, for it was a kind of humour that assumed an English background. As a recitation with music (not as a ballet) it was performed at Siena during the International Festival for Contemporary Music in 1928, Constant Lambert reciting Edith Sitwell's poems, and the Italian audience was positively irritated by it; they did not understand it, but understood enough to begin to fear that they themselves were being laughed at. *The Lord of Burleigh* was another ballet with a definitely English background and the sense of humour that inevitably belonged to it. I could imagine a French audience perhaps appreciating *Les Patineurs*, and *Promenade* still more, for the figure of the entomologist might have come out of Caran d'Ache; but neither Germany nor Italy would have been able to enter into just that charming and delicate combination of the graceful and the grotesque.

In 1937 the Sadler's Wells Ballet was sent over to the Paris Exhibition under the ægis of the British Council; it performed *Checkmate* and other ballets at the Théâtre des Champs Elysées which nearly thirty years before had seen the first European triumphs of the Ballets Russes. The result was more or less what might have been expected; kindly criticisms from the Parisian Press, the friendliest cordiality from French colleagues of the musical and theatrical world, and comparative indifference on the part of the French general public. But the visit to Paris was significant; it meant that the official world in London had had to face the problem of sending some sort of artistic contribution to the exhibition. Our Government (see the Preface to this book) is always reluctant to spend public money on artistic propaganda. On this occasion I think it was well advised; the Ballet really was the best representative art-product that we could at that time offer to the inspection of the world. We have sent so many things to Paris in the past in the hopes of persuading the Continent that we are not quite such barbarians as it thinks: military bands, sometimes even a London orchestra with a thoroughly orthodox Albert Hall programme and perhaps even a Yorkshire chorus as well. We have never yet been able to send over a national English opera company, nor yet a really first-rate Shakespeare company. The actors are here, but just at the moment when they are required for exhibition purposes they are not available. The Sadler's Wells Ballet was not only the most brilliant exponent of theatrical or musical art in the country, it was also the best organised.

If a mere outsider like myself may venture on an opinion, I hope that Miss de Valois and her choreographers will continue to go their own way, inventing rather than reviving, and not paying too much attention to the criticisms of those whose memories are haunted by the past. The connoisseurs are as prickly as theologians, and the English folk dancers and dance-collectors were just as disputatious. The *balletomanes* have become like a religious community, asserting strenuously that they alone hold the true faith universal and that too in a purer form than Paris or Milan, though at the same time they are proud to claim inter-communion with Moscow, and extremely pleased with themselves at having been allowed to celebrate their rite at the altar of the Elysian Fields. But they look loftily down upon the primitive methods of their own country bumpkins, and turn away in horror from the bourgeois dissenters of the flat-footed schools; Geneva is mere pedantry, and for all the various sects of German heresy – Busoni used to say that Germany was always full of little Martin Luthers – they have only that typically English formula of excommunication 'not in very good taste'. *Pruritus disputandi ecclesiæ scabies.*

Chapter Eight   THE SECOND WAR

THE DECLARATION of war on September 3, 1939, threw the whole theatrical world of London into confusion. The authorities had made up their minds that the first thing to be expected would be a systematic bombardment of London and other cities from the air, and all lights in the streets were extinguished after sunset. And since it was feared that bombs would be dropped on theatres and concert-halls causing loss of lives and panic as well, the order was given that all places of public entertainment in which crowds might collect were to be closed. After about a couple of weeks of total darkness a cinema was allowed to open under the strictest super-vision at Aberystwyth, and gradually this permission was extended to cinemas all over the country; theatres, however, were allowed to open only for afternoon per-formances, six o'clock being the official hour of closing. It was, of course, still daylight at that time. Why restrictions should have been removed for the cinemas when they were maintained for the theatres was never made clear; one can only imagine that the cinema industry, being better organised and having more power and influence, was able to get its own way while the theatres remained in a state of hesitation. Managers remembered that the first months of the previous war had been disastrous for the theatre. No theatre could expect to keep going on matinées alone, and during the early period of the war, as in 1914, many people thought it 'not right' to go to places of amusement in wartime; it was only later on, after soldiers began coming home on leave, that the theatre business began to prosper, especially in those theatres devoted to the more frivolous type of entertainment. But as the present war seemed in its initial stages to affect this country very little, there being no battles on a large scale in which British troops were involved, no huge casualty lists every day and consequently no general sense of personal anxiety, the theatres managed to find a way out of the difficulty. They had to begin their performances earlier, as the official closing time was ten o'clock; but by Christmas, 1939, practically all the theatres of London had reopened.

The Old Vic company at the time of the declaration of war was acting at Buxton; although the regulations of the Vic and Wells Trust did not provide for any activities outside London all three companies, drama, opera and ballet, had for some years accepted whatever engagements they could obtain on adequate guarantees in provincial theatres during the summer months. The Governors met on September 15 and expressed their intention to carry on the work of all the companies in spite of financial difficulties. Both theatres had incurred heavy debts, but the members of all the companies agreed to accept greatly reduced salaries. The two theatres were closed and the companies went on tour. When the Board met again a month later it could be reported that the drama company was doing well at Manchester and the ballet company paying its way on tour too. The Vic was closed, and the wardrobe was being eaten by mice; arrangements were made for the storage of it in the country.

Sadler's Wells was in a more difficult position, owing to its greater distance from the centre of London. Ever since it had opened in 1931 it had become increasingly clear that there was really no local public for it, and it was well known that the Old Vic public was not a local public either. Miss Baylis may honestly have believed that in both regions there was a culture-starved proletariat hungering for Shakespeare and Mozart, but in reality both theatres were kept going by a middle-class audience that came from all parts of London and the suburbs. For certain plays and operas, especially if any sort of star was performing, the audience was quite obviously a West End one. The reopening of Sadler's Wells was due not to the initiative of the Governors but to pressure put upon the management by a benefactor who remained anonymous. As an ordinary member of the public he knew that there was a widespread craving for opera and that there were plenty of people willing to face the journey to Sadler's Wells and back even if they had to walk home in the dark. He offered the management a personal guarantee of £250 and after the usual hesitation a matinée performance of *Faust* was advertised for Saturday afternoon, September 30. *Faust* had not been much in the repertory for some years back, but it was the opera which everyone considered safe to draw a popular audience, and it could always be staged with the minimum of rehearsal. On this occasion it filled the theatre to capacity, and the anonymous benefactor made a profit of three shillings and sixpence.

Encouraged by this success, the management continued the Saturday afternoon operas, eventually adding Thursday and Saturday evenings. In December *Otello* was revived and for Christmas *Die Fledermaus* proved a popular success. *Die Fledermaus* is a very suitable opera for a temperance theatre, as its most impressive scene is one which exhibits the revolting spectacle of a drunken man reeling about the stage, a scene hailed by all English audiences with the keenest delight. The ballet company had been on tour with two pianofortes instead of an orchestra; it returned to Sadler's Wells for a month on Boxing Day. At the Vic the drama company had done well with *She Stoops to Conquer*. During the first four months of the next year the theatres continued their activities, but for the theatrical profession in general business could only be described as very moderate. The invasion of Holland and Belgium, followed by the total collapse of France, was naturally ruinous to the theatres. The ballet company at that moment had started on a tour to cover Holland,

1 *Mayor's Reception, Oldham.* [*Photo: 'Oldham Chronicle'.*] 2 *Artists in Welsh Mining Village.* [*Photo: Ministry of Information.*]
3 *Artists outside headquarters in Burnley.* [*Photo: 'Picture Post'.*] 4 *Scenery on the road, South Wales.* [*Photo: Ministry of Information.*]

1 *Rehearsing in a Saloon Bar, Oldham.* [Photo: 'Life'.] 2 *Audience in Miners' Hall, Co. Durham.* [Photo: Ministry of Information.]
3 *Audience in Theatre at Oldham.* [Photo: 'Life'.] 4 *Opera Rehearsal in Court House, Lancaster.* [Photo: 'Lancaster Guardian'.]

1, 2, 3, 4 *Performance of* The Magic Flute *by Elementary School Children.*

1 *and* **2** Richard III, *1944 Season, with Laurence Olivier and Sybil Thorndike.* [*Photos: John Vickers.*] **3** *and* **4** Peer Gynt, *1944 Season, with Ralph Richardson and Sybil Thorndike.* [*Photos: John Vickers.*] **5** *Scene from* Uncle Vanya, *1945 Season.*

[*Photo: John Vickers.*]

Scenes from Peter Grimes, *Re-opening Season of Sadler's Wells, June 7th, 1945.* [*Photos: Angus McBean.*]

Belgium and Paris on behalf of the British Council, but no sooner had they arrived in Holland than they were caught in the German invasion. Thanks to the intervention of our own Legation they were able to escape to England, but they lost the whole of their stock of costumes and scenery. They returned to Sadler's Wells, where both opera and ballet were carried on right into the summer, when they both went on tour again.

In September, 1940, came the long series of heavy air-raids which lasted all through the winter and completely put an end to all theatrical activities in London.

" ..homeless people living in the theatre .. "

The Vic-Wells management found it impossible to conduct business from the Old Vic Theatre, as had been done so far, and transferred the office to Sadler's Wells, but Sadler's Wells, too, very soon became impossible. In the first place it was handed over to the Borough of Finsbury as a refuge for families which had lost their homes by bombardment; secondly, the telephone service became so disorganised that long-distance calls were hardly possible to obtain after about 8 a.m. 'We're a *madhouse:* five tours, either in the country or being organised, and a hundred and sixty homeless people living in the theatre and giving a *lot of trouble*.' The tours were being organised through the co-operation of the newly constituted Council for the

Encouragement of Music and the Arts, now generally known as C.E.M.A. This body had been founded in January, 1940, by the Pilgrim Trust and the then President of the Board of Education, Lord De La Warr, as a private committee to meet the immediate problem caused by the sudden isolation of places in the country, the concentration of workers in new centres, and the collapse of all ordinary sources of theatre and music. Within three months the substantial grant made by the Pilgrim Trust was doubled by the Treasury, and after two years of strenuous work for the organisation of music, drama and the other arts the entire management of the Council was handed over by the Pilgrim Trust to the Treasury, the Council itself remaining the same, a small body of persons nominated by the President of the Board of Education.

The first theatrical company to collaborate with C.E.M.A. was the Old Vic. Rehearsals for its first C.E.M.A. tour in the north of England had begun in July, 1940; the tour itself had already started at Buxton when the air-raids began. The first Governors' meeting after this took place at the New Theatre in St. Martin's Lane by the kind hospitality of Mr. Bronson Albery. 'During the meeting there was a bomb explosion followed by an air-raid warning. [Note the sequence of events.] The Governors moved to the basement to complete the business.' The business was the total suspension of opera and ballet. From Buxton the drama company proceeded to Burnley, where they were received with great enthusiasm, and the same cordiality marked the reception of the opera company a little later. This soon led to the decision of the Governors to transfer the entire headquarters of the Vic and Wells to the Victoria Theatre at Burnley, and the move was effected in a few days towards the end of November, 1940. The Governors had to face the fact that their constitution did not really allow such tours to take place at all, still less that the head-quarters of the two theatres should be removed from London; but they agreed to carry on the work on their own personal guarantees, and as they were assisted both by C.E.M.A. and by the Carnegie Trust, the guarantee was not such a very grave risk to run. There were very soon some four or five drama companies on the road, as well as opera and ballet, performing all over England, Scotland and Wales. The general management of all these tours would have been impossible but for the friendly co-operation of the local committee at Burnley, to whom it was a new excitement as well as a most honourable responsibility to feel that they were now the main centre of dramatic and operatic activity in the country. Mr. Jess Linscott, the managing director of the Victoria Theatre, to whom the Vic and Wells Governors expressed their sincere and cordial gratitude, started off in January, 1941, with a two months' festival: first the opera company with five operas for three weeks; then three weeks of 'classical plays' by the Old Vic companies (note the plural!), which included among their classics not only *Twelfth Night* and *Macbeth* but *Trilby*, an exhumation after so many years that one might almost call it theatrical archæology; finally in the second half of February the ballet with six items.

'BURNLEY, with this combined season of Opera, Drama and Ballet, suddenly becomes the most important creative centre in the English theatre. The event is symptomatic of the times. For too long London and the great metropolitan cities have owned altogether too much of the cultural life of the country. One of the most important and encouraging symptoms of the turmoil which we are at present enduring, is the dispersal of the treasures of art and culture throughout a wider area of the land, and a wider range of the people.

'In London it has been the happiness and pride of the Old Vic and Sadler's Wells to have a personal contact between the audience and the players such as has existed nowhere else; these audiences are famous as the most sternly critical, the most affectionately demonstrative in the world – a real aristocracy of taste and a true democracy of feeling and of manners. It is our belief that a similar potential audience exists here. It is our hope that we shall find it. To please it will be our happiness and pride.'

The joint authors of this prologue, Mr. Tyrone Guthrie and Mr. Jess Linscott, were, as the reader will agree, certainly experts in publicity. If the reader's first reaction is one of amusement, as I dare say it will be, let me beg him to read it through again and to take it quite seriously for a moment, for there are various points in it which he will do well to think over, especially after he has closed the final chapter of this book.

The work of the various tours is only to be described in the actual words of those who directed them. Touring of this kind was a new experience even for the oldest actors, and it meant performing under conditions of every conceivable discomfort and sometimes of positive danger too. The opera company was performing at Hull when the theatre was damaged by a raid; the performers escaped 'by a miracle' but lost fifteen baskets of dresses and properties. The C.E.M.A. tours took the companies to many places which for a generation at least had had no professional entertainment beyond 'the pictures' and exceedingly cheap vaudeville. Most of the people in the audiences had never seen a real play before in their lives. Their reactions to drama were so different from those of London that they suggested an entirely different set of theatrical values, which 'may perhaps be more attuned to the times and more adaptable to the future'. One of the companies went to the mining areas of Wales under the auspices of the Miners' Welfare Association. A tour to cover thirty-eight towns in ten weeks was arranged. The only play acted was *Macbeth*, with costumes of the period of 1745 and scenery consisting of two folding screens and a proscenium. They began at Newport, Abergavenny and Monmouth, but in these towns there was a normal sort of audience, trained up to Shakespeare by the efforts of their own amateurs. At Pengam 'we struck the real thing. There we had the first of those many happy social gatherings, where the local committee, who had organised our visit, welcomed the company with tea, cakes and speeches – and what speakers the Welsh are! The packed house that followed, its silence, its sympathetic attention and enthusiasm, were a foretaste of our reception throughout the tour. Two days there, enjoying the hospitality of the village, then on the following morning, the company in a bus, the staff and scenery in a lorry, driven by the man who designed and painted it, and so on and so on, no town like another, no audience like another, but always the same kindly reception, the same full houses, the same hunger for what we were bringing.

'Sometimes in a Miners' Institute, sometimes in a parish hall, sometimes in a palatial cinema, once or twice even in a theatre. Certain towns stand out in one's memory: Llanhilleth, for its supreme audience; Ebbw Vale, for its charming little hall like an Elizabethan playhouse; Talygarn, where we played on a Sunday on a stage the size of a table-cloth; Treorchy, where the audience sang till we cried with emotion; Maerdy with its singing, its hospitality and its oratory; and Dowlais the derelict with its warm heart.'

Meanwhile the first company was touring in the North. 'The ten weeks' trial was a success, and it was decided to continue after a short break, for one, two and three night stands make strenuous work for the stage staffs in particular as well as for the actors; and most of the places we visited were short of accommodation owing to the starting up of fresh war-industries in the neighbourhoods.

'The success of the Welsh tours which Dame Sybil and Lewis Casson were running had encouraged the Durham and Northumberland Miners' Association to ask if something couldn't be done up there. By March we were ready to tackle it. We had visited the villages to see the halls, and had decided that one of the first considerations in presenting the plays in these bleak dark places must be colour. We thought *Twelfth Night* too sophisticated a play, but they wanted Shakespeare. *The Merchant of Venice* was suggested, a good dramatic story, colourful and easy to follow, linked to a charming fairy-tale.

'It was during this tour that we played in the great hall of Durham Castle. Goodness knows who played there last. Mummers three hundred years ago? No one could tell us!' Ernest Milton was the Shylock for this tour; later on his place was taken by a Czech refugee, Frederick Valk, who had played Shylock in Prague, Vienna and Berlin, but played it for the first time in English at Burnley. He was welcomed enthusiastically wherever he repeated the performance. After the Welsh and North-umbrian tours the companies were brought together again to act *King John* in a larger style of production and in larger theatres. This play went to Paisley, Perth, Glasgow and Edinburgh: after 'two happy weeks in London at the New, rather patronised by critics, but welcomed by old friends', they went on to Bath and finally back to Burnley.

'That one comparatively unknown Shakespeare play should be considered worthy of a whole week was a strange novelty. Nevertheless, the tour was well worth doing. The audiences were always "held" and generally enthusiastic, and I hope appreciated the biting satire on war politics. I think we have at least done something to break down the long-standing tradition that *King John* is dull.'

The tours of the opera company were not quite so exciting, and it must have been horribly depressing for the directors and for all performers to have had to work on such a reduced scale for this difficult period. But like the dramatic companies, the opera people did work of incalculable value in bringing opera, however much simplified and curtailed, to places which had never seen such a thing before. The orchestra was reduced to four – two violins, a clarinet and a violoncello, with Lawrance Collingwood at the pianoforte. Even old Corri might have shuddered at the idea of reducing Mozart and Verdi to that scale. The scenery for *Figaro* con-sisted of two folding screens and one small backless settee. Probably the same properties had to suffice for *La Traviata*. Both operas were cut down drastically and the chorus had to be restricted to two men and two women, who were also understudies if needed, besides looking after the wardrobe, scenery and lighting. The whole company amounted to no more than twenty when they opened at Buxton in October, 1940. By 1941 things were going rather better; there were fourteen principals and a chorus of fourteen, with a permanent orchestra of twenty-three. 'When we are in the Manchester district we augment this orchestra for performances of *Madame Butterfly*, which still draws great audiences.' The repertory in those weeks included *The Beggar's Opera*, which had never been put on at Sadler's Wells. In the north it was received very cordially. *Dido and Æneas* was also put on, with extremely simple but dignified scenery, and Arne's little opera *Thomas and Sally*, though neither of these attracted audiences like *Madame Butterfly*. *Figaro*, however, did well every-where, and so did *The Barber of Seville*, *La Traviata* and *Hänsel and Gretel*.

The Ballet added six new ballets to their repertory during the seasons from September, 1939, to the summer of 1941. For the first year and a half of their touring life they were obliged to content themselves with two pianofortes, but by the summer of 1941 they were doing so well that an orchestra was employed in the big provincial cities where huge audiences could always be counted on. This enabled

Miss de Valois to revive the long classical ballets such as *Coppélia*, *The Swan Lake* and *The Sleeping Beauty*.

The New Theatre had now become the London home of all three companies. The Old Vic was so seriously damaged by enemy action in May, 1941, that the Governors decided to strip the theatre altogether, as it was not considered practicable to repair it and reopen it. Later on it was surveyed by an experienced architect who considered that it might very easily be put into satisfactory condition, all the more since it was found that the theatre was officially scheduled as an 'ancient monument' and the various authorities approached were all very willing to concede it every possible priority as regards building materials. Nothing was done, however, and perhaps in view of the recrudescence of air-raids in 1944 it was a wise decision, all the more so since the L.C.C. had suggested some time before the war that it might be necessary to pull down the theatre altogether to make room for large-scale improvements in that part of London.

The two seasons of 1941-42 and 1942-43 were surprisingly successful, especially as regards opera and ballet. These companies not only paid their own way but made such large profits that they were able to clear off all the debts still outstanding on the two houses and cover the overhead expenses of them. The homeless people were eventually cleared out of Sadler's Wells, and although it was not found practicable to reopen that theatre for performances, mainly owing to the difficulty of getting there and getting away at night under war conditions, it has been in regular use for rehearsals and for storage of scenery, dresses and other property. In November, 1942, a new step was taken by the Drama company; it established a permanent repertory company at the Liverpool Playhouse. This theatre had had a repertory company of its own, second only to the Birmingham Repertory Theatre in the reputation of its achievements, but in 1940 the theatre found itself compelled to close. The new enterprise was not very successful at first, but in the course of a few months the response became more encouraging and the repertory company is now firmly settled there. The Old Vic's other experiments in drama, especially those in London at various theatres, were not so satisfactory; the management attempted too much and it was perhaps a mistaken policy to form *ad hoc* companies, generally round some star actress, for the exploitation of some one particular play, even when the play was not one that might have been taken up by an ordinary commercial management. As the war dragged on the adventure of touring in strange places rather lost its novelty and charm; in all three departments a feeling of weariness set in and there was a very natural hankering after some sort of permanent home. The New Theatre was always available, but it had to be divided between at least three tenants if not more, as the drama department was always ready to increase and multiply. The opera and ballet, so far from increasing, suffered seriously from the demands of the military authorities. Drama can get along at a pinch, as it actually did, with a company consisting mainly of women, and men past military age, for in Shakespeare at any rate there are a good many young men's parts that can be acted by girls. But opera can make no such substitutions, and it cannot depend on the services of elderly singers, though there are plenty going about the country at this moment, in other companies if not in that of Sadler's Wells. The shortage of singers and of other musicians, too, has gravely restricted the work of the opera. Those who are still available have had to do far more work than is desirable, some of them singing every night of the week; actors act every night as a matter of course, but the

exertion of singing an entire opera is much greater and voices are easily liable to be overstrained. Moreover, the shortage of singers has led to a shortage of operas; the great majority of the standard operas were designed for large theatres with enormous resources, and even if orchestral scores can be reduced by the ingenuity of a Corri or a Collingwood, and scenery left largely to the imagination, the number of characters cannot be reduced nor can the chorus in many cases be adequately represented by a force of no more than fourteen. All Wagner's operas are for the present quite out of the question, and a generation is now growing up to whom Wagner on the stage is completely unknown. It will be curious to observe the effect of Wagner on these young people when he returns in full panoply to

the operatic stage, if not at Sadler's Wells, no doubt 'in another place'. Wagner's earlier operas are now over a hundred years old; will they soon begin to sound as remote and classical as the operas of Gluck did to the generation of fifty years ago?

As far back as the 1920's Clive Carey and Geoffrey Toye were insisting firmly on the desirability of basing the Vic and Wells repertory mainly on what the French call *opéra-comique* and the Germans *Spieloper*, opera with spoken dialogue. This did not

mean a lowering of artistic standards in this country, any more than it would in France and Germany, where such operas form a large proportion of the normal repertory. It is obvious, or ought to be, that if *opéra-comique* is represented by such works as *The Marriage of Figaro*, *The Magic Flute*, *The Barber of Seville* and *The Bartered Bride*, it stands on a far higher level than the 'grand opera' represented by *Cavalleria Rusticana*, *Pagliacci*, *La Bohème* and *Madame Butterfly*. The stress of war has forced the Sadler's Wells company more and more to rely upon the former category, and to perform these as comic operas with spoken dialogue in the face of a long-standing and absurd tradition that they are really 'grand operas' of the most conventional and depressing type. Any audience which comes fresh to opera and is not poisoned by the traditions of our grandparents naturally enjoys operas that are amusing as well as melodious and have an intelligible story made fully intelligible by sensible dialogue in plain English instead of dreary recitative in romantic Italian.

From the first revivals in the 1920's *Figaro* and *The Barber* were always acted at Sadler's Wells with spoken dialogue, as they are still in a good many German theatres where spoken dialogue was always adopted in place of Italian *recitative secco*, since spoken dialogue was the normal tradition of the German native stage and the French stage too, as it is on our own since the days of *The Beggar's Opera*. When *The Bartered Bride* was produced at Sadler's Wells some years ago, the original recitatives, or rather, the German arrangements of them, were sung. These were not *secco* recitatives with harpsichord as in Mozart and Rossini, but accompanied by the orchestra; all the same, it must be admitted that they are very dull – they may be acceptable when sung in Czech to a Czech audience, but in any other language they are conventional and tedious. They are also quite unnecessary, and might even have been added as an afterthought, like the spurious recitatives used in this country in *Carmen*, for the songs, duets,

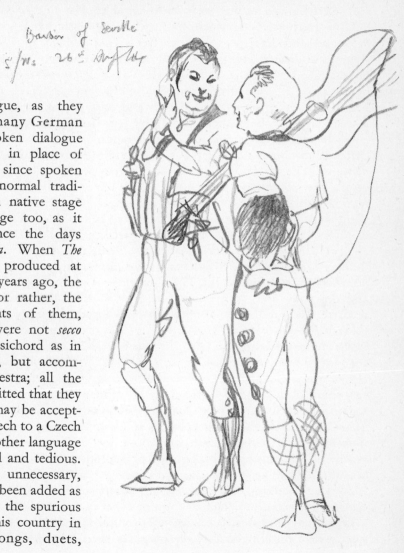

P I

ensembles and choruses of *The Bartered Bride* are all just as clearly separated as those in any of the old French and German comic operas. The first production of the opera at Sadler's Wells was not successful and Miss Baylis removed it from the repertory. When it was considered for a revival in 1943 the management realised that two things were indispensable. The first was a really good ballet. For this purpose the services of a Czech ballet-master were secured by the generous help and encouragement of the Czech Government in London. They released a first-rate dancer who was serving in the Czech army and placed him at the disposal of Sadler's Wells, and Miss de Valois was persuaded to allow some of her pupils as well as one of her front line stars to appear. The Czech dancer trained the English ballet in the national dances and took the principal part himself, with the result that the whole opera was framed in ballet and had that intensely national character which has endeared it to generations of Czech audiences. The other thing that was absolutely necessary was to get rid of the recitatives and substitute spoken dialogue. The whole translation was rewritten by Joan Cross and Eric Crozier, who caught the rather naïve and simple style of the original without ever sinking into the commonplace or the too modern colloquial. *The Bartered Bride* remained what it was meant to be, a genuine folk-opera, and not a 'musical comedy' or 'light opera' in the conventional English theatrical parlance. Of the recent operatic productions and revivals *The Bartered Bride* has undoubtedly been the most successful.

Both *Figaro* and *The Magic Flute* were thoroughly overhauled and studied afresh after the first touring period. The Cambridge Arts Theatre Trust paid for the scenery and costumes and both operas were given their first performances at the Arts Theatre. The production of both was placed in the hands of another refugee dancer, Kurt Jooss. His view of *The Magic Flute* was that as it is a sort of fairy tale it should be permeated all through with the spirit of ballet, and he naturally thought of his own type of ballet, not that of Sadler's Wells. After all, *The Magic Flute* is a German opera, acknowledged by Goethe and by Wagner and many other authorities as the real foundation-stone of German opera; so that to interpret it in terms of an essentially German style of ballet seems to me not at all unreasonable. The Jooss style of ballet suited both the comic episodes and also the hieratic movements of the priests. The high priests of criticism were none too well pleased with it. Some of them resented the intrusion of ballet into opera altogether and maintained that in opera it was the right thing for the chorus to stand in straight lines and do nothing as in the old Italian tradition of a century ago; others resented the Jooss type of movement because they could tolerate no form of ballet except the 'classical'. Audiences on the whole enjoyed the performances thoroughly, but the opera could not be taken everywhere on tour because the choruses needed local augmentation and that was only available in a few places such as Cambridge, where a strong contingent from the University Musical Society gave the choral movements of the opera a singular dignity and beauty. There can be no doubt that Jooss's training was of inestimable value to the whole company; he could show everyone exactly how to stand and walk as well as how to dance, and his insistence on graceful movement from everyone on the stage gave the company entirely new standards of deportment. This was valuable too in the case of *Figaro*, where he made no attempt to 'balletify' the opera, as his detractors would have said, but insisted rather on its political significance. It was interesting also to note that a foreign stage-director took endless trouble to make sure that the singers really understood and made clear the sense of what they had to say or sing. Sadler's Wells on the whole has maintained an unusually high standard of clear enunciation, but there is an inevitable tendency amongst nearly all singers to lapse into unintelligibility, due to their perpetual preoccupation with the technique of voice-production, a technique which one would have expected to become as automatic as that of a first-rate pianist or violinist in the course of years and to be always subordinated as a matter of course to the interpretation of the music.

The hardships of the Ballet are known only to those behind the scenes. Even more than the Opera, the Ballet depends on a copious supply of young men in perfect physical health. They were seized for military service at once, and no efforts on the part of the Governing Body could obtain their release. A few were invalided out of the forces and rejoined the Ballet, but for practical purposes the Ballet was in a perpetual state of uncertainty as to who would be able to dance. New pupils were taken in, some of them highly talented, but this meant an unending series of rehearsals and ceaseless training of beginners. Girls were called up as well as boys. It might have been possible to follow the example of the Shakespeare company in its worst days of difficulty and let some of the girls take male parts; a few in fact did so in *The Bartered Bride*, where the conventions of an operatic ballet made the substitution less noticeable.

But Miss de Valois would never have consented to a return to the old-fashioned 'Empire' practice; it would have ruined the whole character of her ballets. And, indeed, it would have meant completely abandoning many of the ballets which had been most successful, for the new choreography was not designed for 'principal boys'. Chopin (is it meant to be Chopin among his countesses?) can be the one male in the midst of his harem of sylphids, like Parsifal among the flower-maidens and any Prince of Ruritania in the Montmartre cabaret scene of any Viennese musical comedy; but one cannot imagine him represented by a lady of the 'Aladdin' type. None the less, the Ballet continues its existence and continues to produce new works such as *Comus* and *Le Festin de l'Araignée*. Nor is Sadler's Wells the only ballet company to be seen in London; but it is incomparably the best.

*T*O A great many people the fact of living through a period of war is a very convenient excuse for taking no thought for the future. Those who are concerned with the actual management of the three or more Vic-and-Wells companies cannot be blamed if they say that it is all they can do to carry on their daily work of organisation and rehearsal. They have no time for anything else; the conditions of work become more and more difficult every day, and it is hardly possible to make plans for a month ahead because nobody knows who will be available at that date to carry them out. The marvel is that the work still goes on and that the theatres continue to prosper. Among those who have more leisure and perhaps ought to be devoting some of it to thinking out schemes for the future there is inevitably a consciousness of grave responsibility, and that burden leads inevitably to a policy of hesitation. Definite decisions must of necessity be postponed until 'after the war', and no one can give a really definite answer as to what even that phrase exactly means. If in this chapter I venture to discuss some questions of the future, it must be clearly understood that I write on my own private responsibility alone. It would not be at all proper for me to attempt to analyse the ideas of my colleagues on the Governing Body or to outline any schemes which may or may not be under consideration. Even if I did so, any account that I might set down would probably be completely out of date by the time this book is published.

As regards the future of the world in general and this country in particular, it is a commonplace that most people are asking whether we are to try to preserve as much as we can rescue from the ruin of the past, or whether we are to accept its ruin cheerfully and try to build up a new order of things.

It is obvious that we cannot consider the future policy of the Old Vic and Sadler's Wells by itself; that policy must bear some relation to the general theatrical and musical life of the community, and the whole artistic and cultural life of the community will in its turn depend on general economic and social factors. All that I can do here is to set forth some considerations on the future of the two theatres and leave to my readers the problem of relating them to the problems of the country at large. No one, neither our cabinet ministers nor our publicists and journalists, can really deal with all these problems simultaneously. Those who write about 'public affairs' seldom mention the theatre and seem as a rule to be quite unaware of the existence of the whole art of music. But the loyalty and enthusiasm of our audiences, to say nothing of the steady increase in their numbers, are proof enough that there is a considerable body of persons who are seriously concerned with music and drama as indispensable factors in our cultural life, and since these persons are for the most part fairly young, they are precisely the section of the community for whom the future is most important and they are also the persons whose duty it is to take the lead in the shaping and ordering of that future. They may know very little about 'public affairs', but they know what they want; if they do not, then I say to them that it is urgent for them to consider these things and make up their minds. They must not leave things to be settled for them by those who specialise on 'public affairs', whether they stand for vested interests or for a general economic redistribution. People of that sort are sometimes quite willing to give their signatures to an appeal for a National Theatre, but I often wonder whether any of them would ever set foot inside it if it was erected and put into working order.

For the Old Vic and Sadler's Wells the fundamental question is not that of Hamlet, because there can be no doubt whatever that their continuance in some form, and probably their prosperity in any form, can safely be taken for granted. But when the war comes to an end, are they to go back to what they were in 1939 or are they to start a new phase of existence and new spheres of activity? We have seen two complete chapters of their history begun and quite definitely ended, the reign of Miss Cons and the reign of Miss Baylis; we have passed through seven years of a new period which include six years of war-conditions. The war-conditions are not yet finished, and even if the war was to end at once, the war-conditions would to a large extent continue to prevail for some considerable time. I do not know whether I ought to date a new reign from the winter of 1937-38, or whether I ought to regard it merely as an interregnum. Some historians say that the nineteenth century lasted until 1914, and in the same way the historian of the Old Vic and Sadler's Wells might extend the era of Miss Baylis to the end of August, 1939.

Are we to return then, as soon as conditions allow, to the Royal Victoria Hall in Waterloo Road and Sadler's Wells Theatre in Rosebery Avenue, and resume our activities as we left them in 1939? Or are we to change our policy altogether and set to work to become the National Theatre and the National English Opera? If we aim at becoming these, that means that we must take the lead in the entire dramatic and musical life of the country. If we go back to being 'the People's Theatre and the People's Opera' we resign ourselves definitely to a permanently subordinate status and we hand over the leadership to some other body, or it may be to some other individual. Supposing we are humble-minded, what can we do? There are certain people who maintain that everything is laid down for us by the rules of the Charity Commissioners. This is not a question of personal wishes, or personal ambitions, nor even of artistic aims and ideals; it is a legal question and can only be answered by the lawyers. They may very possibly decide that the Governors are legally tied

I*

and bound to the actual bricks and mortar of the two theatres and that we have no right to carry on our activities in any other places. At the moment of writing we occupy the New Theatre and we engage in touring in the provinces; but it is understood that the New Theatre is only a temporary shelter conceded for so long as the Old Vic and Sadler's Wells are unusable. As regards touring, I have already explained the situation, and further to that I may add that a new Trust has now been formed which gives us the legal right to send out touring companies. Under this system we assume the existence of a proletarian audience in Lambeth for classical drama and in Islington for opera, with a similar proletarian audience all over the country. My first instinct is to say that this is all nonsense; the proletarian audience may have existed in the reign of Miss Cons, but from 1919 onwards, if not before, the Shakespeare audience at the Old Vic had become definitely middle-class, and the audience for the opera too, though I can testify that the opera gallery certainly used to include a good many of a more humble class. When I read the accounts of our tours in Wales and Northumbria, extracts from which I quoted in the last chapter, I begin to believe that there certainly does exist a social stratum a good deal lower than that which came to see Shakespeare at the Vic, and that that lower stratum is ready to accept Shakespeare and that therefore it is one of our duties to provide it with suitable performances.

As far as drama is concerned, then, it seems quite clear that there will be an undoubted need for a real *Volksbühne*, a People's Theatre, housed permanently in London, devoting itself mostly to Shakespeare and the English classical theatre, but performing modern plays too, that is, such plays as are not purely commercial in type; and this London theatre ought to be able at the same time to send out a number of subsidiary companies to tour the provinces and especially to act good plays in areas where otherwise probably no plays would ever be acted at all.

But an Old Vic run on these lines would have to content itself from the first with an ensemble devoid of famous stars. Here we come at once to the fundamental difficulty of running any sort of 'idealist' theatre. We must not forget that Miss Baylis started her Shakespeare theatre in the first year of the last war. It so happened that some of her stars were genuinely idealists; but it is safe to say that if there had been no war she would never have been able to collect that particular company. The fact was that the stars were out of work and only too thankful to accept a safe engagement, even at Miss Baylis's scale of salaries; in peacetime they would have been dispersed throughout the West End theatres, acting wherever they happened to find a job. As the dramatic activity of the Old Vic developed, both during the war years and after the war was over, it gradually became clear that Shakespeare could not be repeated *ad infinitum*, and the more modern type of plays would never have filled the house without the attraction of a star or two at least. The best one could hope for would be that in a revived Old Vic such as we are at the moment contemplating new stars would gradually emerge from the permanent school of acting which that theatre would be, and that after they had won their way to fame in other theatres they would occasionally come back to the Vic for a certain period at a nominal salary out of loyalty to 'the old school' and in the same spirit in which eminent physicians and surgeons give their services gratuitously to certain hospitals.

Thus far I have considered the drama alone. Now let us consider the case of opera. Here we shall find that the situation is not altogether the same. A dramatic company at the Vic – I should prefer to call it a Shakespeare company, though I do not thereby mean to imply a strict limitation to Shakespeare alone – could eventually reach a very high standard of performance. Assuming that the West End theatre remained much the same as it has been during living memory, the Vic Shakespeare company would have no competition on its own lines; it would be the only permanent company in London, the only company (apart from Sadler's Wells) with a permanent home of its own. It could in this way build up a great tradition, still more so if, as I suggested just now, its own stars were to feel it their regular duty and pleasure to return from time to time to their original orbit. But a People's Opera established at Sadler's Wells would suffer from a permanent sense of inferiority. If it was in the position held for many years by the *Volksoper* at Vienna when it was conducted by Weingartner (1919-24) it might well feel proud of itself, for it was often said in those days that certain operas were given very much better at the *Volksoper* than at the National Opera. And indeed, if we had a National Opera in English on a level with what the Vienna Imperial and National Opera used to be in its own language, the position of a *Volksoper* at Sadler's Wells might be humble, but it would not be humiliating, as it is bound to be if the old doctrine is revived that Society can be seen only at opera in a foreign language.

If we had a National English Opera, state-subsidized, so as to have no difficulty in maintaining the artistic standards of the great Continental opera houses of former days, then it would always be a noble example to Sadler's Wells, and a place to which the best singers, conductors and stage-managers from the 'lower house' might eventually be promoted. And if, as might possibly happen, the standard of the National Opera were inclined to degenerate into tedious routine, as sometimes happened abroad, Sadler's Wells might perhaps be found giving performances of the same operas with humbler resources but with more intelligence and finish of ensemble. If on the other hand the doors of Covent Garden were to reopen once more to an 'international season', we know what would happen. No doubt all the most marvellous stars in the firmament would be engaged to appear there; how much rehearsing they would do is another matter. And there would always be a certain number of our own singers thankful to be allowed to sing the smallest parts for the sake of the 'prestige' conferred by that historic house, just as all sorts of ridiculous people would be ready to waste their money on boxes and stalls because they think that thereby they would be getting 'into Society'. My left-wing readers, if I have any, will say scornfully that after the present war there won't be any more 'Society'. People said that during the last war, too, and they will say it again during the next. *Plus ça change, plus c'est la même chose*, even if you go back to the days before the French Revolution. Historians may say that I am talking nonsense, but I know the history of opera in this country, however ignorant I may be of economics.*

As regards provincial tours, it is obvious that the Sadler's Wells company, even if it remains no more than a *Volksoper*, ought to be in a position to send at least one company on tour throughout the whole year, unless and until we reach that happy state of affairs when Edinburgh, Glasgow, Manchester, Leeds, Birmingham and other great cities will all have permanent opera companies of their own, like Cologne, Frankfurt and Leipzig. But if the Vic and Wells are to continue functioning merely as People's Theatres, they cannot do so effectively without a state subsidy of some sort. The financial conditions under which Miss Baylis carried on the two theatres were disastrous. Opera is able to make a profit at the present time partly because it is housed in an easily accessible building and still more because expenses are cut down to the lowest endurable limit. At Sadler's Wells in the days of Miss Baylis it was estimated that the theatre could not possibly pay its way unless it was full to absolute capacity at every single performance. No opera house can be run on that system; the last years before the war showed continuous deficits, and if the war had not intervened the theatre would have had to be closed altogether and, indeed, for ever, in default of a subsidy from outside.

Economists may say that it is unsound finance to give performances in a theatre if the receipts cannot possibly cover the expenses. Sadler's Wells replies that a certain artistic standard is a point of honour; it would be unthinkable to return to the age of Corri. But on the other hand the articles of our Trust insist on popular prices, and at these prices the theatre will not hold enough people to bring in the receipts that are necessary. Then why not move into a larger theatre? Even assuming that we could do so, that Drury Lane, for instance, were at our disposal on the same terms as Sadler's Wells; assuming too that we could raise voices adequate to fill it, could

---

* 'One of the *agrémens* of the King's Theatre is the certainty everyone has of meeting his friends from all parts of the world. It is the resort equally of the lovers of music, the dance, and of those who care little for either, but who like to meet each other, and feast their eyes by gazing on all the most beautiful as well as the best dressed women resident in this country.'—John Ebers, *Seven Years of the King's Theatre*, London, 1828.

we be sure that even Drury Lane would pay its way at Old Vic prices? The larger
theatre would inevitably involve greater expenses; a much larger orchestra for one
thing, a larger chorus, more stage staff, and far greater expenditure on scenery.
Then you must build a larger theatre still, with microphones and amplifiers to make
the voices audible all over the house. No; it will not do. I have to admit that I have
never attended concerts in the Hollywood Bowl; but I have attended opera performances in the Roman amphitheatre at Verona, which is said to accommodate 20,000
spectators. It was an interesting experience once in a way, but one cannot face that
sort of monstrosity as the entertainment of every evening, any more than one could
stand a daily repetition of the old Handel Festival in the Crystal Palace. As it is,
opera all over the world has suffered too much already from being housed on too
grandiose a scale.

Accepting for the moment the idea that we should go back to being nothing
more than a People's Theatre and a People's Opera, working on a modest scale for
unsophisticated audiences who cannot afford normal theatre prices, let alone normal
opera prices, are we to accept the legal theory that we are inseparably bound to the
two actual theatres, the Old Vic and Sadler's Wells, or are we to maintain that what
really matters is the moral and artistic ideal embodied in them, not their bricks and
mortar, and that it might be wiser to abandon these sites altogether and continue
our work elsewhere? The fate of the Old Vic will probably be settled for us by the
London County Council. If their new plans for South London are ever carried out,
the Old Vic may be pulled down and another theatre built to replace it somewhere
else. As far as I can gather we may be reasonably certain that every effort would be
made to provide us with a suitable site and a suitable building. The plans which have
been published show a clearly defined intention to develop the whole region between
Westminster Bridge and London Bridge as a centre of educational and artistic
activities. The promoters of the scheme remind us of the glorious days of Shakespeare
when the Borough was the region of the theatre and the entertainment world in
general. That was natural enough in Shakespeare's day, when the relation of the
City to the Borough was more or less that of *Castello e Borgo* as seen even to-day in
many of the older Italian cities. But London has changed more rapidly than any
other European capital, and the topography of its theatres is a curious indication of
its cultural history. The theatres of London are almost all crowded together into
one comparatively small area, so much so indeed that that area is mainly dominated
by the entertainment industry. It has been a commonplace jest for the intelligent
foreigner to discover that the Royal Opera stands in the middle of a vegetable market,
with our other great 'national' theatre just across the road; both of them miles away
from Buckingham Palace and indeed from any wealthy residential quarter, while the

Court Theatre is not a court theatre at all in any sense and is also a solitary exception among our theatres – it is about the smallest of all, and is in the middle of a residential quarter, far away from any other theatre and far away from any other building of cultural significance. New York is the only other great city which has followed London's example in crowding all its theatres into Broadway, as ours are crowded into Shaftesbury Avenue. And Shaftesbury Avenue itself was not laid out until rather more than half a century ago, so that its theatres are all comparatively modern. In Vienna, on the other hand, we shall find the Imperial theatres in the centre of the city, with pretty large theatres distributed through the various suburbs and known still by the names of those suburbs. These are almost all of them old theatres, dating from the eighteenth century, though some have been rebuilt.

I have already mentioned the theatrical plan of Berlin, with its two great state theatres in the centre of the town, close to the royal palace and its commercial theatres springing up in each new quarter that was developed in the course of the last century. But Berlin of modern times shows a difference from Vienna and a sign of resemblance to London and New York; the theatres built since 1918 have tended to crowd the Kurfürstendamm.

Whether the theatre-going public of the future will be willing to seek its entertainments on the Surrey Side once more is a doubtful question. How far the town-planners and architects have given serious thought to the theatre in its practical details is not very apparent from their published plans; it looks as if they had written the word 'theatre' wherever they had an irregular site for which they could find no other use, regardless of whether it was an island site or hemmed in by other buildings, and with no indication whatever of the position and relative proportions of stage and auditorium. Architects are very ingenious people, and they have built theatres on all sorts of curious irregular sites in London and elsewhere; but even those who specialise on theatre-building would seem to have little knowledge of the practical work of the theatre behind the scenes. Sites in the theatrical quarter of London are expensive, and if a theatre is built as a commercial speculation the first requirement is that it should contain the largest possible number of spectators. Their comfort is to some extent considered, for English people will not put up with the conditions that prevail in the older theatres of Paris. The L.C.C. regulations have to be obeyed, but there is always a legal minimum as regards the width of passages and the amount of cloakroom accommodation. When we come to the stage, the actors must just make the best of it. 'Punch has no feelings' said Dr. Johnson to Garrick, and the general public is quite unaware of the difficulties with which all theatrical enterprise has to contend merely for want of space. If the L.C.C. leaves the erection of its Surrey-Side theatres to private enterprise, they will be no better than those which we have already. In any case we may be quite sure that whatever plans are finally accepted by the bodies which have authority to carry them out, it will be several years before any of these projected theatres are built. Our building authorities have erected schools, museums, picture-galleries, possibly even concert halls; the theatre at Stratford-on-Avon is probably the only one in the country which has been carried out by some sort of public body (and that mostly through American generosity), apart from the reconstructions of the Old Vic and Sadler's Wells. And in the meanwhile, what will be the reactions of the owners of the theatres in Shaftesbury Avenue and its neighbourhood to the new theatre-building project?

We shall probably have to assume that if the Old Vic continues its operations as a People's Theatre, it will do so on one of the L.C.C. sites in the Borough, and if an adequate site and a really adequate building is provided, a new Old Vic might well take the lead in developing that whole quarter as an educational and 'recreational' rather than commercial centre of entertainment. Can Sadler's Wells Theatre fulfil the same function? Here we have to face the other aspect of the problem; accepting the principle of two People's Theatres, is it practicable or even desirable to house Shakespeare in Southwark or Lambeth and Opera in Islington? When Sadler's Wells was acquired for reconstruction, it was supposed that it would become 'an Old Vic for North London' performing both drama and opera; after a year or two it was discovered that this was hopelessly impracticable. It may have entered the heads of some of the promoters of that scheme that North London could support a Shakespeare theatre of its own just as well as Lambeth; but I cannot imagine that anybody ever approached the derelict Sadler's Wells site with the idea that here was the ideal situation for The People's Opera House as an opera house and nothing else. All the same, Sadler's Wells, by its own energies, has built itself up such a reputation that it stands a very good chance of being able to carry on its work on that site after the war is over; it is even possible that the theatre, as a People's Opera, would be in itself sufficient attraction to improve the general character of the district as a residential quarter and to encourage the opening of restaurants and tea-shops and various other industries more or less connected with an opera house. But any such hopes must depend first and foremost on the quality of the performances given there, and these equally depend on the amount of subsidy that the theatre may receive. Is this a future which can really be regarded as practicable, or would it be better to abandon the Sadler's Wells site altogether and erect a People's Opera House on one of the L.C.C.'s South Bank sites within easy reach of the supposed new Old Vic and all the other amenities envisaged by the town-planners? Let it be clearly understood that I do not propose a return to the old system under which drama and opera had to work in the same building; that has been tried and is notoriously unsatisfactory. There must be two separate theatres, or possibly two theatres under one roof as at Stuttgart and Munich.

We may now consider the alternative idea of getting the Old Vic and Sadler's Wells established as the National Theatre and the National Opera. At the time of that General Election of 1929 to which I have more than once referred, the idea of a National Theatre was very much in the air. There was less talk of a National Opera, and the National Theatre movement arose out of a scheme for building and endowing what was to be called the National Shakespeare Memorial Theatre. It had been brought forward first in connection with the tercentenary of Shakespeare's death in 1916 and the original idea was that a sum of money should be collected by voluntary contributions to build and to endow a theatre in memory of the poet. Subscriptions came in, but not to any large extent, until Sir Carl Meyer gave a sum of £70,000. With this sum a site was purchased behind the British Museum and it acquired some fame during the last war as the site of what was called the Shakespeare Y.M.C.A. Hut. Some years after the war was over the committee were able to sell this site at a considerable profit, and in addition to that they had considerably augmented their cash balance by the process of compound interest. They were thus able to buy another site which came into the market and which at the time was considered a suitable situation for a National Theatre—a triangular plot of land opposite the main frontage of the Victoria and Albert Museum. Complete plans for a theatre were drawn up by the late Sir Edwin Lutyens and the building might have been erected there by now had it not been for the declaration of war. The site at present is occupied by a static water tank. As to the future I have no official information, but it seems to be generally expected that when the present war comes to an end that site, too, will be sold and the Memorial Theatre erected somewhere else. There seemed to be a fairly general consensus of public opinion that South Kensington was not an appropriate place for a National Theatre.

This theatre, however, whether or not it ever comes into being, would not be a National Theatre in the generally understood sense of the term, because it would be built by private subscribers and its control would no doubt be vested in trustees. It might hope for a Government subsidy, but it could not be at all certain of receiving one. Most people, however, when they talk about a National Theatre or Opera House as a desirable institution for this country, conceive of it as something on the general lines of the National Theatres of the Continent which are State institutions just as much as our own National Gallery or the British Museum. It may be worth our while to look back for a moment and consider how these National Theatres of the Continent came into being. The older ones among them date from the seventeenth and eighteenth centuries, and in every case they began not as playhouses but as opera houses. They were created by emperors and kings, by electors and princes, for the entertainment of themselves and their courts and at first quite definitely for the ceremonial glorification of the monarchy. The Paris Opera dates its foundation from 1672, the Comédie-Française from 1680. In Germany it was another hundred years before the drama was organised as a state institution. The Italian operas were kept going as court functions; it would be difficult to fix an exact date for the establishment of a regular opera performing so many nights a week throughout the year or at least throughout the greater part of it, as opposed to ceremonial operas performed now and then to celebrate some particular event, a marriage, a birth, or just an annual birthday or name-day in the sovereign family. In Germany it was only towards the middle of the eighteenth century that serious theatrical companies were organised. The popular theatre was a sort of *commedia dell' arte;* the Italian comedians did in fact travel everywhere and wherever they went they influenced the local theatre, both in Germany and in France. Troupes of wandering comedians found royal favour here and there and were engaged by the prince, perhaps to stay and entertain him for the whole winter, perhaps to stay on indefinitely with a theatre provided for them to act in; here is the beginning of the National Theatre. It becomes a court institution and its courtly nature is in every case indicated by the arrangement of the seats and standing room; everyone who had the entry to the theatre had his or her proper place assigned in due order of precedence. At Berlin Frederick the Great built the new theatre in 1742 and paid the entire expense of it out of his privy purse; he was a complete autocrat in his own dominions and could dispose of taxation as he pleased. But he was also a public benefactor; he paid for the opera but he threw it open to all his subjects; any respectably dressed person was admitted free to the pit. Frederick was a stout nationalist as far as composers went, and only operas by German composers were performed there; but the words were always in Italian and the singers were mostly Italian too.

Martin Luther, two hundred years earlier, had proclaimed that it was the duty of all kings, princes and great lords to support music for the cultural benefit of their subjects. The Dresden Opera may be said to date from the musical establishment founded at Torgau by the Elector Moritz in 1548. It was at Torgau that the first German opera was performed in 1627; the Electoral court did not make Dresden its residence until later in the century. At Dresden as at Vienna, it is the same story; first the Italian opera, then towards the end of the eighteenth century the settlement of a travelling dramatic company, and not until much later, the establishment of an opera house with performances in German. The political rearrangements which took place in Napoleonic times and afterwards made no difference to the state opera houses and theatres, and the influence of Goethe and Schiller, both keenly interested in the theatre, writers for the theatre and practical directors of theatres, enormously strengthened the position and raised the artistic dignity of the numerous court theatres of Germany. Burney describes Frederick the Great standing in the pit (regularly, at every performance) 'behind the *maestro di capella*, in sight of the score, which he frequently looks at, and indeed performs the part of *director-general* here, as much as of *generalissimo* in the field'. Gustavus III of Sweden wrote opera librettos for his own theatre (as did Frederick too, with the help of an Italian poet or two) and designed his own ballets; in the following century we have the Duke of Saxe-Meiningen undertaking the entire management of his court theatre.

In such countries as Bohemia and Hungary the case is different, because the Emperor Joseph II, in most things an exceptionally liberal-minded monarch, was convinced that the best way of managing his dominions was to impose the German language on all of them. This provoked the resentment of the Czechs and Hungarians and led eventually to the establishment of national theatres for both plays and operas too in the vernacular as a political gesture. In the days of Mozart the local aristocracy at Prague had given employment to Italian comic opera companies; in the days of Weber the German opera was more flourishing at Prague than it ever was at Dresden during his conductorship; it was not until long after that that the Czech national opera became a serious artistic rival to the German opera house.

It is not vitally important in these cases whether the national theatre was established by a princely despot or by a group of ardent nationalists; what is important to note is that in all these cases something was created that was not there before, a theatre – that is, both a building and an organisation – where no theatre previously existed. Secondly, that this theatre, at any rate in German countries, was mainly educational. I hope that my readers will not shy at this word, but will take it in its broadest sense, including that of 'recreational' which I have already used in speaking of the L.C.C.'s policy for South London. If I speak of an 'educational' theatre I do not mean one organised solely in order that school-children may sit through compulsory matinées which count as an afternoon's school attendance, to be followed by the writing of an essay or the answering of an examination paper; I mean that when Frederick the Great built his opera house and threw the pit open to any of his subjects free he was taking thought as a really enlightened monarch for their general cultural welfare. The Czech and Hungarian patriots who started their vernacular theatres were doing exactly the same thing. We are so accustomed in London to seeing dozens of theatres functioning commercially and many of them performing works which the tax authorities have recently classified quite officially as 'educational' that we find it difficult to conceive of a capital in which the king plants down a 'real theatre' performing 'educational' plays or operas because previously there has been seen there little more than a sort of magnified *Punch and Judy* acted by casual strolling companies. Lastly, the fact that the national playhouse of the nineteenth century had been preceded by perhaps a century or more of a dynastic opera house eventually burdened most of the national theatres with the operatic tradition of sumptuousness and magnificence. Covent Garden opera, for even the oldest of those now alive, calls up only memories of shabbiness and absurdity on the spectacular side, however excellent it may have been as regards singing and orchestral playing. We contrasted it contemptuously with the lavish decoration, as well as with the technical ingenuity and efficiency, of many of the other theatres in London. But in other countries it has always been the opera which took the lead in spectacle, from seventeenth-century Venice to the German courts of the eighteenth century, to Meyerbeer and Dr. Véron in Paris of the nineteenth and to Berlin and Dresden in the twentieth. Indeed, in the days of Purcell and Handel, it was the same in this country; it has been shown that it was quite usual for playhouses to buy the discarded scenery of the opera and use it for some totally different entertainment.

In England we have had to do everything for ourselves. If we started a national theatre to-day we are not in the same situation as those who started a national Hebrew playhouse and Hebrew opera at Tel Aviv. We have managed our own theatres without either royal or parliamentary help or interference for so many centuries that many people now view with profound mistrust the idea of a state-supported theatre either for drama or for opera. In 1929 the magazine *Drama* asked a large number of prominent people for their views on this question; as one might expect, the irresponsible bohemians of literary and artistic circles demanded it with loud cries. The higher up the question was put in official strata, the more discreetly noncommittal were the answers. The following example is typical:

'Lord Crewe regrets he has not had any opportunity for studying the different proposals for establishing a National Theatre in London, but he thinks that a carefully-thought-out scheme should receive general support if framed on a sound financial basis.'

The noble Marquis, we observe, is the only correspondent who replies to Mr. Geoffrey Whitworth's question in the third person. The Duke of Wellington would at least have had the courtesy to present his compliments too.

As regards practical policy to be adopted after the present war comes to an end, it has been suggested that it would be advisable to unite in a common effort the resources of the Shakespeare Memorial Theatre, the Stratford-on-Avon theatre and the Old Vic; if all these three worked jointly under one management, it would be a great saving of expense and would simplify the whole practical organisation. Whether the three bodies concerned would agree to such an arrangement I have no knowledge. Among those who sent their views to *Drama* in December, 1929, there were the enthusiasts from outside the theatre who simply wanted a National Theatre and a National Opera and were content to say no more than that; the people who spoke from inside the theatre were apt to be more cautious. There was always a haunting dread of bureaucracy and officialdom, leading to utter stagnation, and there was also the perpetual fear that the theatre might 'get into the hands of a clique'. When people use that phrase what they really mean is that the theatre may come to be dominated by some personality with whom they themselves have no sympathy, and a personality with a quite definite policy of its own.

There are various policies which a National Theatre might pursue; it might even succeed in combining them, however incompatible they might seem to be. We might say that our first business is education, and stand for a strictly orthodox repertory of the Shakespeare plays which are read regularly in schools, with a few other standard classics – roughly speaking, a repertory to which no one could ever take exception on moral grounds. Others might press for the systematic performance of old plays which are not considered practicable for the commercial theatre at all: that the National Theatre ought to continue the work done hitherto by the Marlowe Society at Cambridge and the short-lived Phœnix Society in London. Against this it might be argued that the National Theatre is not intended for 'museum pieces'; such pieces are more appropriately presented on special occasions such as drama festivals, research congresses and so forth, and the most suitable settings for them are the universities, which ought to be places of pilgrimage for those who are interested in dramatic exhumations, just as Stratford is obviously a place of pilgrimage for schools and for young people on the threshold of Shakespearean appreciation. Dare we suggest that the National Theatre ought to be pre-eminently a theatre of experiment, a theatre in which all sorts of new and courageous methods of presentation – whether for Shakespeare or for any other author – might be tried out? Another idea suggested is that it should make a point of reviving all sorts of plays of the last half century or so, plays by living or recently deceased authors, plays that were considered quite good in their day but have not been revived because their authors have continually produced new plays for us. This type of repertory would really mean an attempt to give these plays the canonical standing of 'classics'. At present the 'classics' end with Sheridan; are they always to end there? A National Theatre might at any rate try the experiment and see whether it can create classics or not.

Most important of all will be the attitude of the National Theatre towards entirely new plays, and especially towards entirely new playwrights. Here the economic factor at once becomes critical. The man who is already at the top of the tree – and posterity may eventually say that he was a really great playwright as well as a gigantically successful one – will probably avoid the National Theatre altogether. His income depends on a long run, a run of a year or more, with all sorts of possible film rights to be considered too; will he consider it such an honour to be brought out at the National Theatre that he will accept the comparatively small fees that it will be able to pay him, and the few performances – perhaps a week's run – that its unwritten law will allow it to give? The National Theatre must obviously be a repertory theatre with a stock company, but it seems to be quite impossible in this country to adopt the repertory system of the French and German theatres, and the system of all opera houses – to perform a different work every night. This does not preclude repeating a successful work once a week, or even twice or three times. The state-subsidized theatres in Germany have always worked on a subscription basis, at any rate for the last hundred years or so; but this assumed a permanent population of people so much interested in the drama or in opera that they were delighted to go to the theatre regularly once a week if not more. This has never been possible in London except for the Italian Opera. I have no statistics available, but I should imagine that even at Covent Garden the number of regular subscribers was a good deal smaller in the present century than it was in the days of Queen Victoria. Miss Baylis always maintained firmly that a subscription system at the Old Vic (I speak of the days before Sadler's Wells was opened) was utterly impossible, although if ever there was a theatre in London that depended on faithful and regular devotees it was her own.*

There is more precedent here for running opera on a subscription system, but Miss Baylis always regarded that too as impracticable, and she was probably right. We have always to remember that theatrical and musical conditions in London to-day are not those of Dresden fifty years ago. In a small town where life was tranquil and distractions few it was for every middle-class family quite an event to go regularly to the opera or the theatre – the same theatre, too – once a week; it was like going to church on Sunday. In London all theatres depend on the variable population; permanent residents do go to the theatre, some very often, but there are so many to choose from and there are so many different distractions of all kinds that no one would want to tie themselves down to weekly attendance at one only.

* At the moment of writing a modified repertory system is being tried by the Old Vic at the New Theatre and by Mr. John Gielgud at the Haymarket as well. Three plays are acted at each theatre, by the same company, so arranged that there is a different play each night, This is 'repertory'; but as it is a repertory of three plays only, the real fact is that at each theatre three plays are being acted concurrently for long runs.

The future of opera in this country – by which, I need hardly say, I mean opera in English – is certainly a good deal less precarious than it has been in the past. The granting of a state subsidy would really be a much more reasonable thing in the case of opera than in that of drama, if it is once admitted that opera in itself is as legitimate and desirable a form of entertainment as drama without music, for we have plenty of drama going on all the year round while opera at this moment is confined to occasional visits of the Sadler's Wells company when not on tour in the provinces. Other performances of opera are too irregular and uncertain to take into consideration. If the establishment of a 'Shakespeare' theatre – i.e. a classical repertory theatre – is justifiable on national grounds as something which we have hitherto never possessed, the claims are even stronger for an English opera house.

Stanford pointed out many years ago that without a national opera house it is useless to train up singers at our national schools of music. The chief difficulty with which English opera has to contend at present is the shortage of singers who are adequately trained for dramatic work. This shortage was apparent long before the beginning of the present war, although of course the conditions of war have made it worse than ever. Some people have suggested that the only solution of this problem is the establishment of a separate opera school, such as actually was carried on by the Carl Rosa company for a short period; others would make for some sort of agreement between the opera establishment and the existing schools. Into the relative merits of these schemes I do not propose to enter. But it is obvious that if any opera director were to approach any director of a music school on the question of operatic training, as things stand at present, or as they stood in 1939, the inevitable reply would be that opera, either English or not, offered no safe career to a student of singing, even to the most highly talented. For one 'People's Opera House' in London there are hundreds of choral societies up and down the country offering engagements to sing *Messiah* or *Elijah*. The singer need only learn a very small repertory of works far less exhausting than any operatic parts and his living is assured; he will be paid a higher fee for a single oratorio than he would earn for any operatic performance. Nor is it any good to suggest that an operatic connection is a good advertisement to a singer. Not even Covent Garden confers upon him the prestige (in oratorio circles) that he would enjoy and retain from having his name painted up in large letters outside the Albert Hall.

We find ourselves therefore in a vicious circle; opera cannot make headway until it gets the singers, and the singers will not study for opera because opera can offer no career. This is obviously the moment at which the State might well step in and provide a subsidy in the form of scholarships for opera students even if it was unwilling to subsidize opera itself to any great extent.

A few pages back I mentioned the long-standing tradition of operatic magnificence. That conception of opera will in the immediate future have to be regarded as out of date. A good deal of that historic sumptuousness has now passed to the cinema and opera may be thankful to be rid of it. When it comes to making estimates for a season's expenses it may be questioned whether the outlay on scenery and costumes, even on the scale of the last half century, is actually greater than the ever-increasing cost of the modern orchestra. In the reign of George IV Madame Pasta was paid at the rate of about a hundred guineas a performance; that was probably more than the cost of the entire opera band for that night. In these days we are all glad to think that the orchestral player receives a stipend more adequate to his artistic abilities and his social position; as to the *prima donna* we can only hope that her reign of terror is over. On the other hand there is not much hope for the future of opera in any language if the general tendency of composers to neglect the vocal interest altogether for that of the instruments is pursued much further; yet as I write these words I am obliged to remind myself that the same laments were made in the days of Mozart and Handel and in those of Scarlatti and Monteverdi as well. The composers of the future will have to settle affairs with the public of the future; the business of the historian is merely to record and not to offer advice.

There may be readers who will accuse me of having neglected the ballet in this discussion or future developments. The ballet is at this moment so completely the spoiled child of the family that its exclusive devotees may well expect it to survive as the unique theatrical art of the future after drama and opera have long passed into oblivion. The historian may be a little sceptical; if there is any lesson to be learned from stage history it would seem to be that the three sisters have passed through various phases of unity and separation and that they will probably continue to remain associated, since it is clearly to the advantage of all three – yes, even to spoken drama – that they should remain in friendly relations. For the practical needs of the moment, this association of all three under the same general direction, as under Miss Baylis, is obviously satisfactory; but in any case, whatever practical and economic rearrangements the future may bring, the principle of friendly co-operation and friendly interest in one another, not by the 'three sisters' alone but by all their supporters and well-wishers too, is to be encouraged.

On no account should ballet and opera become permanently separated. At this moment they tend to diverge; ballet proceeds on its own delightful path and opera gets along without it as best it can. The same thing was happening in the reign of George IV, not particularly in London, because London in those days simply took over what it could borrow from Paris and Milan or Naples; it was the general tendency in the great opera houses to have short operas and long ballets. Fashion changed, and the elaborate ballet became more of an integral item in the spectacular opera; that again passed away with the mature Wagner and his German followers. But the practical convenience of sharing an orchestra ought naturally to keep ballet and opera together, even if they co-operate no more closely than that; and if the English opera composer of the future wants a ballet, he will be able to enrich his work with choreographic subtleties of which Meyerbeer and even Wagner in his Venusberg never dreamed. The lamentable fact is that opera, certainly in this country, and in other countries as well, as far as can be judged, has come to a dead end; there is no other way of describing the situation. Sadler's Wells still lives on the remains of a nineteenth century repertory; Paris, Berlin and New York, judging by the state of affairs before the war started, were really in little better case. The safe repertory ended with Puccini; there were a dozen or more operas that were supposed to have made history and which certainly ought some day to be restored to the position that they deserve – I will name only one out of many – *Pelléas et Mélisande*. But the fact remains that they are all as risky from the box-office point of view as are the museum operas of the past. Perhaps they really are museum operas of the past, and we ought to face that fact. They were experiments in their day; I cannot bear to class them as failures. But we stand more than ever in need of operatic experiments, and here the ballet can help us, just because at this moment it is far more advanced than opera is.

And that is why the question of a 'people's opera' or a 'royal opera' is less urgent than the definite permanent establishment of an 'English' opera in which our own composers can try out their experiments. At the present moment they do not seem much inclined to try operatic experiments or even to take any interest in opera at all; they are either stuck in the mud of oratorio and cantata or they allow themselves to be seduced by the cinema and the wireless. One of the greatest advantages of the ballet is that it cannot be broadcast; the cinema appears to have no use for it either, and that leads me to hope that television will not take very much notice of it. A ballet can only be itself; there is no *Ersatz* for it. We need it indeed at this moment, because the ballet is the one musical form that has become popular on a basis of modern music. Opera in the past has depended all too much on great voices; if they had been allied to great personalities they might have carried opera forward instead of perpetually holding it back. Modern critics, not unjustly, hold the *prima donna* of the old days up to scorn, but in the exaltation of the conductor which has followed this reaction they have reached the last depth of absurdity. The opera of the future, at any rate in this country, will probably have to practise a rigid economy in orchestral resources; there is every probability that for some years to come we shall hear no very outstandingly beautiful and powerful voices. We shall have to depend more than ever on team-work and intelligence, to appeal to the understanding rather than to desire to escape from intellect. The ballet and the opera must enter into a new partnership. A hundred years ago the ballet was no more than the humble servant of her elder sister; we may find it desirable that she should for a time become the predominant partner.

Berlin, in the prosperous days – artistically and intellectually prosperous at any rate, if not financially – between these last two wars, was able – and without a crowned head's privy purse – to maintain three opera houses on the largest scale simultaneously. Between the repertories and the general standards of the three there was not much difference, judging on a long-term view. Two were maintained by the State in succession to the monarchy, the third by the municipality. At Vienna there was the State opera on the grand scale, and there had been various short-lived seasons of popular opera at the *Volksoper*, but as the State opera in recent times depended largely on the support of foreigners, and the population of Vienna really preferred entertainment of the 'musical comedy' type, the *Volksoper* never established itself as a permanent institution. In smaller German capitals such as Munich and Stuttgart there were two adjacent theatres subsidized by the State, one large and one small, used alternatively by drama and opera. On one night there might be *Julius Cæsar* at the large theatre and *The Marriage of Figaro* at the small one, or *Charley's Aunt* in the small house and *Aida* in the large one. In Paris there were the *grand opéra* and the *opéra-comique*, devoted to large and small operas respectively, with other theatres for State-subsidized drama.

What ought we to aim at establishing in London? From my experience of the Old Vic and Sadler's Wells I fear that the joint tenancy of adjacent large and small theatres, convenient as it may be for towns the size of Munich and Stuttgart, is not practicable for us in London. Drama and opera ought to have their separate homes. Some day, perhaps, we might hope to see four State subsidized theatres, large and small, two for drama and two for opera; but since it is fantastic to expect the Government to build us even one theatre within the next five or ten years, we must resign ourselves to making the best of what accommodation is already in existence. As regards drama there are plenty of theatres of various sizes; for opera the problem is more difficult because of the necessity of finding room for a full orchestra. That is why it is urgent that a new opera-house, with all adequate space for operatic requirements, should be the first theatre to be built by some public authority. It may very well be that the Old Vic Theatre will have to be pulled down to make room for new street plans, and that a new People's Theatre may be built in the projected 'welfare centre' on the south bank of the Thames.

We might then ask ourselves whether we want to see erected a pair of opera houses, one for large operas and the other for small, both functioning, as at Paris, on the same sort of artistic level, with appropriate prices of admission, or whether we shall return to the idea of two opera houses, one for the rich and the other for the poor. But I think that the democratic reader need not take fright even at this last alternative, for if we ever got as far as running two opera houses, they would in practice arrive at much the same result. The large house would be forced to charge higher prices, in view of the expenses of opera on the Wagnerian scale, and the small house could keep its prices down and perhaps be more attractive to popular audiences by a choice of repertory such as its dimensions would naturally impose.

At the present moment there is such a shortage of singers, and indeed of every other thing that is necessary to operatic enterprise, that it will be necessary for us to make every effort to concentrate all energies on one opera house alone and raise that to the highest practicable standard. I need hardly say that I take it for granted that this one opera house must be a truly National Opera, with all performances in our own language, except for occasional visits from foreign ensembles. We must have no more of the old Covent Garden system of engaging the stars from a dozen different foreign countries and allowing them to sing, without any sort of serious rehearsal or stage-production, in what they may be pleased to call Italian, or even, as I have heard in the past, to sing French operas in German, and German operas perhaps in a mixture of Italian and French. Anything, in fact, as long as it is not English! And if foreign singers are invited to join our English company singly, it must be on a long-term contract, and on the clear understanding that they sing in English and rehearse regularly like their English colleagues. There must be no repetition of the old contracts such as were made with Pasta and Patti in the past, whereby these ladies had the right to direct rehearsals, but were exempted from all obligation to attend them.

Lastly, it must never be forgotten that both in opera and in drama we have now discovered the immense range of our duty to provincial audiences. The difficulties of the war years have at least shown us the urgent importance of bringing both opera and drama to places where such things have perhaps hardly ever been seen or heard before. In developing our provincial tours we are educating new audiences to an understanding and love of the real theatre, and this is a problem of daily increasing urgency in view of the gigantic influence of the cinema all over the world. The cinema threatens to destroy the living theatre altogether; many of us fear that a time may come when the living theatre will exist only as a highly specialised entertainment for a small coterie of intellectuals, or may even cease to exist at all. There are millions of young people in England now to whom it is natural and normal to go to the cinema as often as they can afford it, perhaps once a week or more; how often do they enter a real theatre? In many cases never. On the other hand the enormous development of amateur acting since the foundation of the British Drama League in 1919 must have developed a general stimulus towards the theatre the value of which it is difficult to assess. Broadcasting is another dangerous competitor which has encouraged many people to sit quietly at home and listen – probably with very easily distracted minds – to all sorts of spurious drama; on the other hand it may be argued that broadcast drama and broadcast opera do something to create a desire to see the real thing with one's own eyes.

Another aspect of both drama and opera is the desirability of providing both these things for audiences of children. Children are taught to act plays, and have even been encouraged to act operas; but there is a considerable difference between seeing other people act a play or opera and joining with one's friends to act it oneself, a difference which is possibly more vital to the child mind than to the adult. The subject of a children's theatre – already developed on a large scale in Russia, as one might expect – is too large to be pursued here; all I can do is to invite the reader to think it over for himself.

If the Old Vic and Sadler's Wells are to become truly national theatres they must achieve that status, subsidized or not, by their own creative efforts and the public's whole-hearted acknowledgment of them. Hitherto all operatic effort in this country, native or foreign, and most dramatic effort too, has aimed no higher than the imitation of something that somebody has already seen and admired somewhere else. This is not enough; we shall achieve nothing unless we set ourselves aims and standards which we have never seen and which exist only in our own imagination. Whatever of real cultural value the Old Vic and Sadler's Wells have so far achieved between them has been the result not of commercial routine but of the enthusiasms of idealists and visionaries. It is in their hands that the future of the British theatre lies.

BIBLIOGRAPHY

BAKER, H. Barton. History of the London Stage. Second Edition, London, 1904.

BAYLIS, Lilian and HAMILTON, Cicely. The Old Vic. London, 1926.

BELL, E. Moberly. Octavia Hill, a biography. London, 1942.

BOOTH, John. The Old Vic. London, 1917.

CRAIG, Edward Gordon. Henry Irving. London, 1930.

FAGG, Edwin. The Old 'Old Vic', or, from Barrymore to Baylis. London, 1936.

FAGG, Edwin. Old 'Sadler's Wells'. London, 1935. (Published by the Vic-Wells Association.)

FOSS, George R. What the Author meant. London, 1932.

FILON, Augustin. Le Théâtre Anglais. Paris, 1896.

HAZLITT, W. A View of the English Stage. London, 1895.

HOLLINGSHEAD, John. My Lifetime. London, 1895.

HUNT, Leigh. Critical Essays on the Performers of the London Theatres. London, 1807.

MACREADY, W. C. Reminiscences, edited by Sir Frederick Pollock. London, 1875.

NICOLL, Allardyce. A History of Early Nineteenth Century Drama, 1800-1850. Cambridge, 1930.

NICOLL, Allardyce. The Development of the Theatre. London, 1927.

ODELL, G. C. D. Shakespeare from Betterton to Irving. London, 1921.

POEL, William, and his Stage Productions, 1880-1932. London, 1932.

POEL, William. Shakespeare in the Theatre, 1913.

POEL, William. What is wrong with the Stage? London, 1920.

PÜCKLER-MUSKAU, Prince. A Tour in England, Ireland and France in 1828 and 1829. London, 1832.

SCOTT, Clement. The Drama of Yesterday and To-day. London, 1899.

THE ANNUAL REGISTER. London, 1940-44.

THORNDIKE, Sybil and Russell. Lilian Baylis. London, 1938.

WESTWOOD, Doris. These Players, a Diary of the Old Vic. London, 1926.

WHYTE, Frederic. Actors of the Century. London, 1898.

WILKINSON, Tate. The Wandering Patentee, or a History of the Yorkshire Theatres from 1770 to the present time. York, 1795.

WILLIAMS, E. G. Harcourt. Four Years at the Old Vic. London, 1935.